understanding

The Simplicity of Life

Winner in the "US Indie Excellence Book Awards,"
in the category, New Age Non Fiction

Finalist in the "Next Generation Indie Awards"
in the category Spirituality.

Finalist in the "US National Best Books Awards,"
in the categories,
Eastern Religion, New Age Non Fiction and,
Interior Design and Layout. (David Dalton & Michelle Keir of onedesign, Courtenay, BC. Canada.)

Books by the author

Something To Ponder,
reflections from Lao Tzu's Tao Te Ching

Winner
US National Best Books Awards
Eastern Religion 2009

Winner
International Book Awards
Eastern Religion 2010

Finalist
National Indies Excellence Awards
Interior book design 2010

...

Like a large immovable rock,
a Festschrift in appreciation of the Advaita Master,
Ramesh S. Balsekar.

understanding

The Simplicity of Life

Colin Mallard, Ph.D.

Understanding

The simplicity of life

by

Colin Mallard, Ph.D.

Promontory Press
ISBN: 978-1-927559-03-1

First Edition: September 2010
This Edition: September 2012

Cover design and layout by
Dave Dalton & Michelle Keir of onedesign,
Courtenay, British Columbia, Canada
dave@onedesigncom.com

Photographs by Colin Mallard
colinmallard.com

Original cover photo by Mel Brackstone

Printed in Canada
www.promontorypress.com

In appreciation of:

Dr. Wilbur Mullen
Who introduced me to Socrates,
challenged me with ideas and showed
me the importance of an unfettered mind

Dr. Cecil Paul and Dr. Ron Gray
Whose love of truth shone like a beacon
from beyond the limitations of belief

To Dr. Jean Klein
The Advaita master par excellence
who pointed at the moon

And
to the beloved Advaita master
Ramesh S. Balsekar
who opened my eyes

Thank you Kate Jones and Tress Backhouse
For reading the manuscript and offering suggestions.
Your help was invaluable.

Thank you David for the cover design and layout. You have created the perfect setting for what follows.

A special thanks to Val Walton, my editor and friend, without whom this book would not be what it is.

I met Ramesh Balsekar in the autumn of 1990 at Hermosa Beach, California. That meeting changed my life. I'd gone to India in January of that year in search of "someone who knew," someone who could answer my questions.

After that initial meeting I traveled to India for the next twenty years. Ramesh was my guru and you will meet him in the pages that follow. I mention this only so that you, the reader, will have some idea of whom it is I speak when mentioning his name.

Ramesh died in September 2009.

Colin Mallard.

***Note:** Throughout this book the masculine tense is used but refers to all human beings both male and female.*

Introduction

I first read Colin's book, *The Examined Life*, partly out of intellectual curiosity and partly out of a desire not to be as cynical about religion and all things spiritual. I've started so many books which promised a great deal only to be disappointed. This book, however, gave me more than I expected, guiding me through the complexities of a totally different way of thinking, and therefore, living.

Although I loved the ideas I felt I was moving away from life, a kind of withdrawal to a serene almost self centered space. Then my circumstances changed drastically and I discovered this serene space was in fact a place of strength giving me power to adapt to and enjoy life despite the difficulties. I found I could look at problems directly without apportioning praise or blame as I used to. I was able to deal with the difficulties as they arose, and to stop worrying about what might happen, or what, given the benefit of hindsight, I should have done. I was introduced to the gift of living in the present!

Colin answered my questions with incredible patience and one day I realized he'd become my teacher. After all I was far too old, middle class and respectable to have a guru. Besides, that would have made me a disciple. I finally worked it out—the difference between a guru and a teacher, that is—A teacher helps his pupil acquire knowledge while a guru does the opposite. A guru helps strip away the accumulated conditioning from both cultural and personal sources and thus enables one to awaken to life as it is.

Colin has been helping people for a number of years, answering their questions and mine. The book you are now reading emerged from this process. *Understanding*, is a replacement, not a sequel to the earlier book, *The Examined Life.*

Val Walton

The Great Way is not difficult
for those who have no preferences.
When love and hate are both absent
everything becomes clear and undisguised.
Make the smallest distinction, however,
and heaven and earth are set infinitely apart.

Sengstan (3rd Zen Patriarch)

When holiness is discarded and religion done away with
People are much better off.
When morality and justice are forgotten
People do what is natural.
When the idea of profit disappears
Theft comes to an end.

Lao Tzu

Chapter 1
To Begin With

Empty your cup

Professor Daniel Robertson taught Eastern Religion at Harvard University. His specialty was Zen, and after thirty years and twelve books the professor was considered an expert in the field. He'd never been to Japan, however, so with a sabbatical coming, he decided to go and visit the well-known Zen Master Hakuin. Shortly after arriving in Japan he made his way to Hakuin's temple. He rang the bell and a small elderly monk appeared. Dr. Robertson explained the nature of his visit and said he had an appointment to see Master Hakuin. The monk took him through the garden to a gazebo where he was told to wait. A few minutes later Master Hakuin came through the garden and, entering the gazebo, bowed to his guest. In perfect English he welcomed the professor. They sat opposite each other, a small table between them. Hakuin asked the guest if he would like tea. "I would," said Dr. Robertson. The master rang a bell, and when the elderly monk appeared, he was asked to bring tea.

"Tell me what brings you here and how can I help," Hakuin said in a clear and quiet voice. Dr. Robertson described in detail the start of his career—how, as a student at Harvard, he had been approached to come on staff once he graduated; and how very pleased he was to have been invited at such a young age.

The professor told Hakuin about the books he'd written, the many students he'd taught, and the numerous awards he'd been given. He then went on to tell Hakuin about a series of guest lectures he'd recently completed and how well received they'd been. As the tea arrived and was placed on the table between them, the professor continued to describe his achievements. Hakuin took the pot of tea and started pouring into the cup which sat on a delicate saucer on a black lacquered tray. Dr. Robertson noticed that Hakuin continued to pour the tea until it was overflowing the cup and the saucer and beginning to spill onto the tray. "Stop, stop," he shouted, "the cup is too full!" Hakuin put the teapot down and, looking at the eminent professor, said, "You have come to see me, but, like this cup, you are too full. Until you empty your cup how can you receive what I have to offer?" *(Zen story)*

• • • James

James, a clerk in a local shoe store, earned just enough to get by. He enjoyed the people he worked for and the customers he served. He lived at the end of a long lane lined with a hedge of dense cedars a couple of miles from town. At the end was a cottage, his home for the past fifty years. It was a small cottage with only one large room. The inside was clean and cared for by someone with simple tastes and few needs.

James rode a bicycle to work in the morning and home again in the evening. On weekends he could be found in the garden that surrounded the cottage on three sides. The back of the cottage was attached to an old brick wall some thirty feet tall and covered with wisteria. The cottage itself was set at the back of a large open landscaped area covering about ten acres.

Every so often James liked to walk along a trail that led through a dense forest, where it intersected a path running at right angles. On one side of the path was a canal that stretched in both directions as far as the eye could see. On the other side of the path was a four-foot wall that surrounded a beautiful estate. By turning to his right he could walk between the canal and the wall. About a mile along the wall, two widely separated stone pillars marked the entrance to a long driveway that wound its way through gently sloping fields to a large and secluded mansion visible through a stand of tall beech trees. The setting was exquisite and James often wondered who lived there. Over the years he'd never met his reclusive neighbor. He had, from time to time, however, seen a gardener who attended the shrubs, pruned the trees and obviously took care of the grounds.

James had lived in the cottage since he was a young man. Following the death of his parents he inherited the property on condition that he was never to open the door at the back of the cottage. He never had.

Viewed from the inside, the back door was no different from the front door. At times he found himself wondering just where the door might lead and what was behind it. Being an obedient and somewhat timid man, James had never opened it.

One evening after supper James sat alone, feet propped in front of the fireplace where flames flickered around a large log. He found himself looking at the door and wondering what was on the other side. A couple of evenings later, when he returned from the garden, he thought he heard a noise coming from the other side of the door. He held his breath and listened intently. He must have been mistaken; all was quiet. Throughout this particular week he found himself wondering more and more about the door and what was on the other side. As the weekend approached, his curiosity got the better of him. He'd wait until his day off on Saturday, then he would open the door and explore what was on the other side.

Saturday morning arrived, and after breakfast James approached the door. He turned the handle and slowly pushed it open. With an initial creak, the heavy door opened smoothly. He found himself in a beautiful hallway lined with small colonnades that supported flowers and delicate marble statues. His attention was drawn to a number of paintings which hung on the walls along the hall. He'd never seen such beauty before. The floor, of ebony parquet, shone with a warm and inviting glow. Halfway down the hall James turned into a large and elegantly appointed living room. A fresh fire burned in a large fireplace. Hearing a sound behind him, James spun around as a butler entered the room. Surprise and recognition spread across the old man's face and his dancing eyes were warm and friendly.

Before James could say a word he heard the butler saying, "Welcome home, Master. I've been waiting for you. How wonderful to see you again." Surprised by the man's words, James replied, "There must be some mistake; I'm not the master of anything and this is certainly not my home."

"Ah, yes, I understand. You must have forgotten, but this is your home. You are, indeed, the master of this house and I am your servant. It's been a long time since you were last here, but I would know you anywhere."

After showing James around the house the butler took him outside to see the grounds. As they walked through the gardens James noticed an old man pruning a tree. There was something familiar about him. As they approached, the gardener looked up and a lovely smile spread over his face. "You've come at last," he said, and his blue eyes sparkled with delight. Suddenly, as if waking from a dream, James realized the gardener was the man he'd seen on his walks along the canal. Then it struck him: where he now stood was in front of that same mansion, and his cottage was simply another entrance.

The butler put a hand on James' shoulder. "Yes," he said with a smile on his face, "you live here; the mansion is yours! Welcome home." It was then that James remembered everything.

True words are not necessarily eloquent
Eloquent words are not necessarily true.
Lao Tzu

Chapter 2

Words Are Not The Truth

Some thoughts on language

Traps are to catch rabbits
And when that is done
Traps are forgotten
Nets are to catch fish
And when that is done
Nets are forgotten
Words are to convey
That which lies behind them
And when that is done
Words are forgotten.
Chiang Tzu

The Advaita master Ramesh Balsekar was fond of saying, "My words are not the truth." What he meant was that words are nothing more than concepts that point to the truth. Truth is truth; the concepts about truth are still just concepts and therefore not the truth. Many are familiar with the image of the Zen master pointing at the moon and his students standing looking at his finger. What the master wanted was for them to look beyond his finger and see the moon.

Language by its nature is subjective. What someone understands by the words I use may not be what I mean, because their understanding of key words is different from mine. In the material that follows I will attempt to define words clearly to make it easier for the reader to understand exactly what is being said.

And, hopefully, by the end of the book the words will no longer have any significance because that to which they point will be understood; the reader will understand the truth for himself.

Metaphors

Metaphors are guideposts, pointers, ways of looking—glimpses through a fence, so to speak. They're helpful but ought not to be taken too literally. This book is full of metaphors, stories and anecdotes, so keep this qualification in mind.

The concept of God

When the term God is used in this book, it is simply a convenience of language. It is just a concept, as nothing really can be said about God. In mathematics "X" is a symbol used to represent the unknown. Despite the fact that X is unknown, it is possible to use it in an equation in such a way as to obtain a sense of that which is unknown. God is really just a symbol for the unknown, much as X is a symbol in mathematics.

Lao Tzu uses the term, "the Tao," and goes on to say that:

The Tao that is spoken
Is not the eternal Tao.
The named
Is not the eternal name.
The nameless is the source of all names
And the named the source of the ten thousand things.

Mystery wrapped in mystery
The Great Tao dreams
And life takes form.

In Judaism the name for God has the vowels removed in order to render it unspeakable, whereas in Buddhism there is no direct name for God and "the Void" is used instead. It can also be referred to as the Great Mystery, the Totality of Consciousness, Potential Energy and the Source. When reading the word "God" in this book it is helpful to keep these concepts in mind.

• • • The nature of understanding

To understand life it is not necessary
To know a great deal
No need to look at the world through a microscope
Or the heavens through a telescope
Much learning gets in the way
And the more one knows the less one understands.
Lao Tzu

. . . . .

When the European mariners understood that the world was not flat, their behavior changed simply as a result of their understanding. Despite their fear they began to sail out of sight of land and not one of them fell over the edge.

In learning, something is added. We actively engage in learning in order to acquire something that will give us a benefit or advantage in life, or simply because we're curious. Understanding is something completely different. Nothing can be done to bring it about. Understanding has its own time frame, and simply happens when the right conditions prevail. Understanding is something that comes upon us at the most unexpected of times. We experience it usually with the exclamation, "Of course!" Archimedes ran through the streets of Athens shouting, "Eureka, I have found it!" after sitting in a bath and realizing how he could determine the volume of an object. Einstein had worked on the theory of relativity for a long time when the understanding dawned on him. He was gracious enough to recognize that the insight "came from outside" himself. Fritz Perls referred to these spontaneous occurrences with the German word Gestalt, which means to see as a whole.

Spiritual awakening is direct understanding of a spiritual nature. Sometimes it comes in small increments that take place over extended periods of time which, in the end, contribute to a much larger, all-encompassing realization, known as enlightenment. In other instances the understanding can be immense and profound—one sudden cataclysmic realization—with the same result. It is for this reason that the experience of awakening appears, on the surface, to differ so much from person to person.

When understanding does take place, however, it is preceded by a peculiar kind of attitude. This attitude is one where the mind is open, and is accompanied by a willingness to surrender preconceived notions and abandon beliefs in the interest of truth. This openness is often accompanied by the acceptance that neither the activity of the mind nor spiritual discipline can bring about the understanding the seeker wants. It could be said that to know God requires the abandonment of any belief in God. This state of mind, this attitude, is variously referred to in Zen as the "beginner's mind," the "fasting mind," or the "vacant mind."

To read what follows, it is helpful to approach it with a beginner's mind. What this means is to understand as clearly as possible what is being said. It is not helpful to argue with what is presented because to do so demonstrates attachment to one's ideas, one's preconceived notions or beliefs. It is not being suggested, however, that you believe what is being said, but rather read with the idea of fully comprehending it. Once an intellectual understanding takes place the mind will come up with plenty of questions—"Yes, but . . ." or, "If this is the case then what about . . .?" Such a response is to be expected and welcomed; this is the "right use of the mind," a term used in Zen.

Having travelled this way myself, I was able to ask all the questions that arose in my mind and to hear the same and other questions that arose in other minds. As it turns out, all minds are the same in their underlying structure and function, although the content and conditioning is different from person to person. As a result the spectrum of questions arising is also more or less the same. Consequently an attempt will be made in this book to address all the typical questions that arise. It is suggested, however, that you do not settle for accepting what is said without first testing these things in your own life. Do not believe what I have to say, as it will prove useless for you. To reiterate: If you can approach the reading of this book with an open mind, prepared to surrender your preconceived notions and beliefs; when you have fully comprehended what is being said, and examine closely what you've understood against your life experiences, then you may come to know the truth for yourself.

Description and prescription

Ramesh makes an important distinction between description and prescription. Christ is reported to have said, "Love your enemies, do good to those who despitefully use you..." This sounds very much like a command to do something, a prescription for behavior. A prescription is an appeal for action, an appeal to the ego. All spiritual disciplines are prescriptions.

A description is quite different. If we take Christ's statement and turn it into a description, which I think is the correct way to take it, it would read as follows: "When you love your enemies, when you do good to those who despitefully use you . . ."

Description fosters understanding; it brings spontaneous changes in behavior and does not expand the ego. A prescription is found in the statement, "Don't step over the balcony," which sounds like an order, challenge or threat. It is this reactive tendency that is the basis for reverse psychology. To describe gravity is much more beneficial, as no one feels threatened or challenged. "If you step over the balcony you will fall fifty feet," is a description and so it doesn't provoke the ego to defend itself or to prove it is an exception to natural law.

In the story of the Garden of Eden, God is reputed to have forbidden Adam and Eve from eating the fruit of the tree of the knowledge of good and evil. The original reverse psychology! A direct challenge to the ego brings predictable results. Adam couldn't help himself; his curiosity, and the forbidden nature of what he wanted to do, guaranteed what happened.

Throughout this book you'll find considerable use of the passive voice, since the passive voice is a description. The active voice suggests a command and is usually perceived as a challenge to the ego. What is said in this book is not a prescription for anything. What is presented is a description based on observation.

The difference between belief and truth

Let's come back to the word truth. There's a definition of truth found in both science and philosophy which states that truth is self-evident. That is, we recognize it as fact, simply so. When the word "truth" is used in this book, this is what is being talked about. Truth is not something learned; it is not abstract and something that must be believed; it is simply a fact. So for instance, the fact that two Canada geese just swooped low between the trees and landed in the pond is a fact. There's nothing esoteric about it. Anyone present could testify to the obvious. What then is the difference between belief and truth? The answer provides an important distinction. What is central to all belief? This concept can be illustrated by the following story. Pay attention to what happens in your mind with this scenario.

A man, who was an intense spiritual seeker, was troubled by the issue of suffering, the resolution of which became an obsession. He needed clarification on the issue; it was driving him nuts. In conversation with a friend he mentions his concern and lack of resolution. His friend tells him he's just heard that Zen master Po is in town and happens to be speaking on the topic of suffering. He shows him a flier, which he reads carefully. There's a number to call to reserve a place. He calls and gives his name to the woman who answers. She tells him the session will be held at ten o'clock the following morning at the meditation house of a nearby retreat centre. The next morning he arrives in town early and stops at a local coffee shop. While sitting at the table reading a newspaper, he meets a friend who asks why he's in town. He explains he's come to hear Master Po. The friend looks at him doubtfully and tells him there's no such person and there's no session being held at the retreat centre. This man is someone he's known for many years, a fellow seeker, a person known for his truthfulness.

Now, let's take a slightly different scenario. It starts the same as the first one. A man calls to confirm a place at the retreat centre. The next morning he arrives in town in just enough time to make it to the centre before the meeting with Master Po. He spends two hours with Master Po and is able to ask questions and get some guidance on the topic of suffering. What a relief! After the session he thanks the Master and leaves. Stopping at the coffee shop he thinks about the conversation with Master Po. A good friend comes in and asks what brings him to town. When he tells him, the friend looks at him in a strange manner and says there's no such person as Master Po. Look carefully . . . what happens? What is the difference between what takes place in the mind with the first scenario and this one?

In the first one when his friend tells him that Master Po doesn't exist, doubt enters because he really didn't know, having never met him, and his friend is known for his honesty. In the second instance he's already met Master Po, so he knows he exists. This time when his friend says Master Po doesn't exist, he looks at his friend quizzically but there's no doubt in his mind concerning Master Po. There may be doubt as to his friend's sanity but certainly not about the existence of Master Po.

What is central to all belief is doubt, not knowing, uncertainty, ignorance. When it comes to truth, however, there's no uncertainty; something is simply recognized as being true. Now this is not to say that what is believed may not be true also; but the believer will never know that what he believes is true. In addition, one of the characteristics of belief is that it seems to take on weight by numbers. Among those who believe there's the idea that if enough people believe it, it must be true. This is why those who believe, such as those who attend a church, temple or mosque, often try to convert others to their set of beliefs. Since they don't really know, since doubt exists, there's an attempt to obscure the doubt with the idea that if enough people believe it, it must be true; they couldn't all be wrong. However, that is not the case. For a long time there was a belief that black people were inferior to white people. It didn't make it true. Hitler tried to get the German people to believe the Jews were not really human. Some sects of Judaism believe that about the Gentiles. Many Muslims and Christians believe they have the final, exclusive, and true revelation of God. None of these beliefs make them true. The fact there are so many conflicting beliefs in the world should produce skepticism as to their truthfulness.

When belief is challenged, those who believe may become frightened, consider themselves under attack, and in extreme cases become violent. Who they take themselves to be has become deeply entwined with their beliefs. In fact who they are is largely defined by those beliefs. But belief is essentially empty and not a place for certainty. When I enter a restaurant and look at a menu with pictures of the food, it helps me select what I want. I believe the pictures accurately represent the food I will receive. They may or may not. But, I'm not satisfied with the menu itself. I know it's not real and I want the real thing, I want the food. Belief is the menu, truth the meal; and for the spiritual seeker simply to believe in God is insufficient.

To use the personal consciousness
To return to the Impersonal Consciousness
Is the beginning of wisdom.
Lao Tzu

Chapter 3

The Impersonal Consciousness & The Ego

From the womb of consciousness

At the moment of birth the infant responds to sensory input, to sound and touch in particular. After several days it begins to focus its eyes and to follow movement. If we ask the question, "Is the child conscious?" we would have to say, "Yes." But, when we ask the question, "Does the child have personal consciousness—that is, does it respond to its name and know itself as separate and unique?" the answer would have to be, "No."

It is clear that the infant upon birth does have consciousness, but the consciousness is impersonal in nature. As the infant begins to focus its eyes it has begun the process of discerning between objects as separate from the general background, from each other and from itself. The same discernment takes place with hearing, touch and smell. At this point the infant has begun to identify objects from their background. This learning in its early stages is pre-verbal. In Buddhist terms it is referred to as the "endarkenment process." In the West it is known as the "acculturation process," which means learning the cues and fundamental assumptions concerning the human being, language, society, and culture.

• • • The impersonal consciousness and the personal consciousness

With the passage of time the infant is called by name—let's say, Johnny. Johnny may demonstrate a natural artistic ability and a poor mathematical ability, and his parents will tell him many times that he is good at art and poor at mathematics. There are three things being learned here. One, that Johnny is good at art. Two, that Johnny is poor at math. Three, and most importantly, that the consciousness associated with a particular body has a specific name associated with it (in this case, Johnny). As the association with the name and body takes hold, the acculturation process can be said to be well under way. The association of the name and body is essential in the development of the sense of personal consciousness; what is commonly referred to as the ego, or personal identity. This ability to distinguish between objects also means that the child begins to see its own body as an object of perception. In the early stages of this development the identification with the body is still tenuous, and as a result the child can be heard to say, "This is Johnny's leg," "This is Johnny's nose," "Johnny has a tummy ache," and so on. When the personal consciousness has become firmly established the child will say, "This is my leg," "This is my nose," and "I have a stomach ache." The shift in language from third-person to first-person reflects a movement from impersonal to personal awareness.

It is interesting to note that when the same impersonal perception returns in adults and comes to the attention of psychiatrists and psychologists, it can be labeled "dissociative" behavior and considered a form of mental illness. In certain shamanic traditions this characteristic is highly valued and in some instances brought about intentionally through training. The process that leads to awakening is a reversal of the identification with the personal consciousness. As the hold of the ego becomes more tenuous, the shift to the impersonal awareness is sometimes reflected in language when the impersonal third-person perspective is used again.

It must be kept in mind that the development of the personal or identified consciousness is conceptual in nature, as distinguished from the impersonal consciousness, which remains the underlying consciousness from which the personal consciousness is derived. Perhaps a metaphor might be helpful here. Air can be said to have no intrinsic shape. However, when a bottle is opened air enters and assumes the shape of the bottle. The underlying characteristics of air remain the same however, despite the container that now encloses it. The impersonal consciousness, like air, has no shape and represents our original nature.

What do I know for sure?

To understand the difference between personal and impersonal awareness more clearly, answer for yourself the questions, "What do I know for sure?" "What do I know that is not a belief?" Some might answer, "I am my body," or "I am a carpenter, a teacher, an intellectual, or a mechanic." While these may in a sense be true, they're not what we know for sure; in fact they're secondary in nature. When we stay with the question long enough we eventually arrive at the understanding that in order to know, for instance, that I am a carpenter, something else would have to be true, something else would have to exist. What is it that would have to exist to know I am a carpenter, to know my name, or to be capable of perceiving objects?

What about the idea that I am my body? If I slap you on the back of the hand it will hurt. You might look at me and ask, "Why did you hurt *my* hand?" When I look at *my* leg, *my* hand, *my* chest, *my* torso, these represent different parts of *my* body. But who is it that says it is *my* body? Although we may not be able to answer the question, we all know that whatever we perceive, we are not. Think about it for a moment. When I look at a tree I know I am not the tree. It, like my body, is an object of perception and hence not what I am. The same is true of my thoughts, my patterns of behavior. When I recognize the thoughts or patterns of behavior, I obviously cannot be them.

We're looking for something known in philosophy as a priori, or that which must exist prior to something else; that which is essential and without which nothing else could exist. To know I am a carpenter or a teacher is secondary. To know I have a body is secondary as well, derived from something else, and that something else would have to be existence or consciousness itself. Without consciousness there could be no awareness of being a teacher or having a body.

So, to answer the question, "What do I know for sure?" I would have to answer, "I am." What then is meant by "I am?" Is it not the sense of presence, the sense of being, of being alive, consciousness itself? The fact that I am is incontrovertible. I exist; I am aware of being. This is quite different from my belief that the sun will rise tomorrow. The awareness of being, of "I am", is a priori; it is beyond all belief and concepts. The Advaita sage Nisargadatta Maharaj said that the only coin of any real value the human being has is the sense of presence, I am.

The birth of the ego

If one examines closely the difference between "I am," and "I am Johnny" or "I am Karen," it becomes clear that "I am" is the underlying consciousness, the impersonal consciousness, the consciousness not shaped by the name and story associated with a particular body. In the development of the personal consciousness we weave a story largely derived from our family, which in turn is set within a particular society, a particular nation and a particular culture. In this story, which can be called the ego's story, we find ourselves playing two roles, the role of hero and the role of victim.

As events occur in life we find our minds recounting the stories heard from our parents and others important in our lives. In those stories we're engaged in a struggle against overwhelming odds, against circumstances beyond our control, against events that demonstrate an intrinsic unfairness. If we're successful in our encounter with these events, we look upon ourselves as having waged a heroic struggle and emerged, relatively speaking, victorious. If, on the other hand, and despite our heroic struggle, we are overcome, then we find ourselves recounting the story of our victimization, which will often be reflected and reinforced by those around us.

When we walk into a room filled with people, the mind can often engage in an assessment of who can be trusted, who we like and who we dislike. We generally consider others less important than ourselves. There's a particular process sometimes used in psychodrama that points this out beautifully. Participants are told to form themselves into a single line numbered from one to ten. One is close to the group leader and ten is the furthest away. There's no value placed on the numbers and no talking allowed. Participants in the group automatically assume that "one" is the most important position and "ten" the least important. They will attempt to place themselves in the higher-ranking positions, and tension and conflict result. What lies behind this tension? The sense of self-importance, the ego. Sometimes this is reversed in some who feel inadequate, those whose experiences were exceptionally negative and undermined their perceived value as human beings. But, even in these participants it is still the ego functioning. The ego must make us out to be important by either being the greatest or the worst. We could be the greatest person we know; or we could drive a Harley, wear a beard, have a big belly and be the "meanest dude" that ever walked the earth. No matter how it is expressed, positively or negatively, it is still the inevitable function of the ego.

The collective ego

There are also national stories of the ego, stories that reflect our national identity. For those who grew up in England during the Second World War, there's the heroic story of how the population of a tiny island stood alone against the might and power of the German war machine and contributed to the fall of the Third Reich. The Russians, on the other hand, remember the invasion attempts of Napoleon and Hitler, the subsequent massive deaths of the Russian people, and the ultimate defeat of the invading armies. For the Jews during the Second World War we have the stories surrounding the Holocaust and the desperate struggle to survive horrifying conditions. Today, many of the national stories have been combined with certain religious overtones. For example, the Al Qaeda leader Osama bin Laden has identified with the story of oppressed Muslims encountering the destructive self-interest of Western nations such as those in North America and Europe. These events he's linked to the oppression of Muslims by the invading Christian armies of the Crusades and the destruction of high Muslim culture, with its mathematical and scientific contributions to humankind. The Americans have their own story. They consider the United States to be a "city on a hill," a beacon of light and hope for the oppressed of the world. Some American leaders have seen themselves as the bringers of democracy to the Arab world. Canadians see themselves as peacekeepers, nicer than the rest of the world, definitely not American and proud of it.

At the heart of these stories, as in the case of our family and personal stories, lies the belief that we are right and others wrong. This is simply the collective ploy of the ego, which pits one person or one group against another.

When this takes place, each believes they are right, even going so far as to express the belief that God is on their side. This is as far from true spiritual understanding as one can get. When this kind of thinking is combined with a literal interpretation of scriptures it becomes a recipe for disaster and a great deal of suffering.

At present we have a looming shadow of misunderstanding that suggests a conflict of epic proportions between the Christian West and the Muslim East. If we encountered space ships landing on earth we would forget our differences and align ourselves against another perceived threat. The ego always divides the world into two groups. One group consists of those who are with us—our friends, relatives, fellow countrymen, and fellow believers; on the opposing side are those who are not like us, those who disagree with us, those we don't like, those of another nationality, color or planet . . . our enemies. There's nothing right or wrong in any of this; it is simply the way things work, and anyone who takes the time to rigorously examine human society and his own life will be able to confirm it.

On a more personal level—the matrix of the ego

The following story will help describe the matrix—the pattern of the ego. I returned to Hawaii after being away for ten months in an attempt to market a book I'd written. I was glad to be home but as time passed I felt an increasing tension with my wife. Late one afternoon we found ourselves in a full-blown argument. Disgusted with myself, I loaded the dogs in the truck and drove to a small lane that led to some cliffs overlooking the ocean. I let the dogs out of the truck and we began the two-mile walk to the place where the surf crashed. I was so upset I even yelled at the dogs: everything annoyed me.

I found myself wondering what it was that precipitated these conflicts. As I walked it suddenly dawned on me that the ego is a matrix—that is a repetitive pattern which is predictable in nature and always has the same objective. As I thought about it I could hear a typical dialogue, one with which I was also familiar from conversations with clients who came for counseling. It seems we had all read the same script. What follows is a common scenario.

"All right, lets get to the bottom of this so we don't have to deal with it again."

"Sounds good. How about you starting."

"All right. Yesterday, when you said . . . I felt so upset and angry with you I wanted to leave. What you said was unwarranted."

"That's true, but in the morning before leaving for work you said . . ."

"I didn't say that. That might be what you heard but it certainly isn't what I said."

"I have a good memory, I remember it clearly. Anyway what you did about three weeks ago was completely inappropriate. You didn't treat me with respect . . ."

The dialogue, if that's what it could be called, was predictable and repetitive and never resolved anything. As it went on it became more heated, and anger, like lava, flowed just beneath the surface.

What was behind it all, what was the mechanism? It would have to be the ego. The ego always wanted to be right, it always wanted to win and always portrayed the other person as somehow wrong, even someone I loved as much as my wife. I continued to examine the process, trying to find the underlying cause. When I looked closely it was clear the underlying cause was my wife. If we could go far enough back it would be obvious that she was the first cause. She, on the other hand, felt the same way. That is, if we could go far enough back she would discover the first cause and that would have to be her husband, me.

I wandered along the cliffs as the dogs ran free, the trade winds blew and the big waves curled, shedding foam to the wind before crashing against the rocky shore. The ego lies, I thought. I always think in some ways I'm better than others, and they think the same in reverse. Neither is true. As a way of speaking it could be said that in the presence of God, all human beings are of equal value. None is better or worse than any other. But that is not what the ego would have us believe. Obviously the ego lies. Now if someone lied to me and had done so all my life, why should I believe him? I would be a fool to do so. Yet for how many years have I believed the lies spun by the ego?

When I look at people, they are all unique; their behavior, mannerisms and characteristics are all different. Yet beneath the differences the matrix of the ego is the same; it lies to us and would have us believe that our actions are selfless, that we are the repository of truth while those with whom we find ourselves in conflict are somehow flawed, selfish, dishonest and responsible for our difficulties.

What a web of illusion and self-righteous arrogance the ego weaves. Not only does it enmesh others, it also enmeshes us. But how can we see this when we are so focused on the perceived shortcomings of the other person?

If I tell you that you have a flat tire when it's not true, it doesn't matter if you take the car to the garage, as they cannot repair something that doesn't need repairing. A false problem can never be resolved. The ego often creates false problems and no amount of trying to resolve them can work. The problems are simply not real; they never existed in the first place.

Understanding this dynamic proved helpful, to a point. Conflict between us was usually ego-driven, and once it took place there was no sense expending effort to resolve it. It was a false problem, one that really did not exist. Months later I found myself in the middle of a full-blown disagreement with my wife. I could feel the buildup of tension and knew at once what was happening. It was relatively easy to let it go, to realize it meant nothing.

When beauty is considered
Ugliness comes into being.
When good arises, bad is present as well.

Being and non-being arise together
Difficult and easy are a pair
Long and short define each other
That which is high rests on that which is low
Sound arises from silence
And afterward always follows before.

These are complementary opposites
And one cannot exist without the other
Such is the nature of life.

Lao Tzu

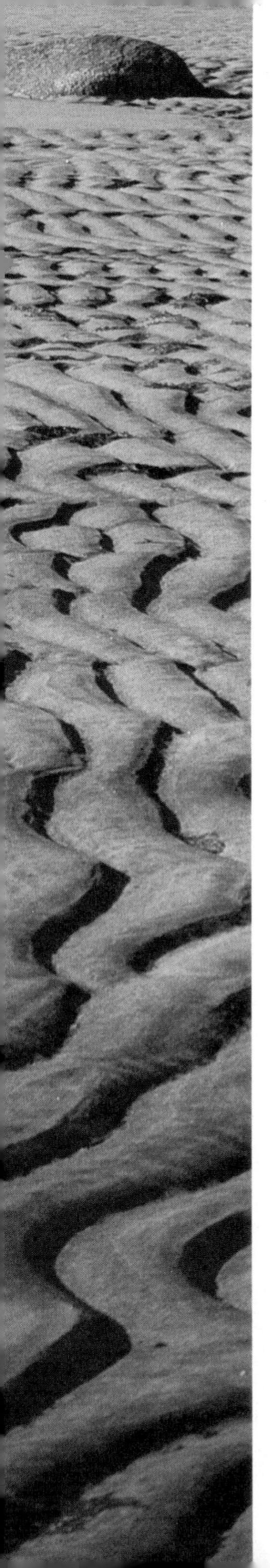

Chapter 4
Duality & Dualism

The concept of duality

The concept of duality is important. For instance, if we look at a rock, what enables us to see the rock are two characteristics essential to perception in the phenomenal world, the world of objects: namely, its presence and absence. If we took a rock and extended it into infinity, there would be no end and no beginning and hence no rock. This characteristic of presence and absence enables all objects to be perceived by the senses. The smell of a rose is distinguished from that which is not the smell of a rose. If there was only the smell of a rose there would be no ability to make the required distinction, and hence the unique characteristics associated with the smell of a rose would be absent. By the same token, sound and silence complement each other, as does touch and its absence. The concept of beauty is meaningless in the absence of its opposite, ugliness. Good and bad are also complementary opposites and do not exist in isolation. Duality reflects the nature of things, so it is an important aspect of the human ability to perceive the objects of manifestation in the phenomenal world around us. It is also important in enabling us to understand those concepts that do not exist in isolation.

In the Taoist symbol of yin and yang the opposites are represented as being in harmony with one another. In addition, in the black aspect of the symbol can be found a white dot and in the white aspect a black dot. This design represents the concept that in each aspect of duality the opposite also resides. For instance we know that a certain amount of control is required in driving a car to make driving safe and fluid. If control is taken to an extreme, however, it makes driving unsafe and less fluid. Control and its absence must therefore come into a harmonious and flexible tension for driving to take place safely. A corrupt political party may be thrown out of office. The opposition party takes over and implements changes to restore integrity. After a while the new party may become proud of its accomplishments, complacency giving way to arrogance; and before long it too may become corrupt and the cycle of replacing parties continues.

Duality and dualism

As was mentioned, duality reflects the nature of things and enables us to function in the phenomenal and conceptual world. The phenomenal world is the world of form, the world of things or objects, the world in which we live. The conceptual world refers to the world of ideas and language. When we look at a coin we see on one side what we refer to as the head, while on the other side we see what we refer to as the tail. When we toss the coin repeatedly it would be foolish to expect only the head to show up, without the tail. The head and tail go together; they are two sides of the same coin. The same is true of beauty and ugliness, good and bad; they go together and do not exist in isolation.

In dualism there's a misunderstanding of reality, an attempt to have the one and not the other, the head but not the tail, the good to the exclusion of the bad. In Christian and Islamic culture we've been conditioned to dualism. That is, we are taught to strive for the good and to negate the bad. Even the concept of God in these religions is perceived as dualism because of another concept called the Devil. We are taught that we must strive for God and seek to escape the clutches of the Devil. When awakening takes place the misunderstanding is resolved and there's a return to the awareness of duality.

In Advaita Vedanta, and Taoism, for instance, dualism is understood for what it is. In religions that practice and teach dualism there's a perpetual frustration because no matter how hard the person tries to be good, bad is there as well; it's impossible to escape. The yin-yang symbol depicts the essential polar opposites as being in harmony. So from the perspective of Taoism, for instance, it is understood that peace of mind is not found in achieving the good and negating the bad; peace comes about when the good and bad tendencies balance each other. When this occurs they cancel each other out and what remains is the silent centre of harmony, the harmony of opposites at rest.

Seeing the world from the perspective of duality tends to give rise to peace, whereas the dualism of Christianity, Islam and Judaism gives rise to polarization, conflict, violence and war, as exemplified in the Middle East.

There is no greater suffering than attachment
No greater foolishness
Than not knowing one has enough
No greater misfortune
Than wanting what others have.

He who knows he has enough
Finds peace
His mind is no longer disturbed.

Lao Tzu

Chapter

The Source Of All Suffering

The source of all suffering

Children born without the sensory ability to distinguish between hot and cold are at risk for burns. Most people who put their hands on something hot experience pain and an immediate involuntary reaction to pull their hands away. This is part of the normal safety mechanism of the body. When walking through the woods enjoying the bright colors of spring and the sweet scent of cottonwood, I suddenly experience a sharp pain in the bottom of my foot. Immediately the awareness shifts from the flowers and the smell of cottonwood to the pain. I stepped on a nail, which went through the shoe and into the foot. Having understood the source of pain I take the necessary action to remedy the problem.

Pain, then, is natural, necessary and important. It serves as a warning that something is wrong; the body is at risk. Pain draws attention to the source of the pain and prompts a response to correct the problem. In as much as pain functions in the body, suffering functions in the mind and serves a similar purpose.

What then, is the cause of all suffering?

Let us examine a number of events and see if it's possible to extract the underlying cause of suffering common to all of them. I've been visiting relatives in Hawaii and have to return to Canada Tuesday evening, which begins with a local flight to Honolulu. Knowing I need to be at Keahole airport at 7 p.m., I leave Kohala at 4 p.m., intending to stop and have supper in Kwaihae. I arrive in Kwaihae to find my favorite restaurant closed. I'm not happy; I'm disappointed. I decide to go to Kamuela to have supper in another favorite restaurant. I tell myself, hopefully, that there should be plenty of time. After supper I look at my watch and realize I have to move quickly to get to the airport in time to return the rental car. About two miles from the airport I'm pulled over for speeding. I'm even unhappier now. I accept the ticket and get underway. Arriving at the rental agency, I'm processed quickly but then have to wait for the bus to take me to the ticket counter. Once more, I find myself upset. Things are not going as expected and now I might miss the plane. Finally the bus comes and in fifteen minutes my bags and I arrive at the ticket counter. I've only a few minutes to board. I'm informed by an official at the ticket counter that my plane has been delayed. Now I'm really upset. With the local flight delayed I've missed the flight to Canada. Re-booking will be expensive and I'm pissed off.

Let's try another scenario. I'm nine years old and Christmas is coming. I've seen a bicycle in a store. I pass it on my way to and from school. To my mind it's one of the coolest bikes I've ever seen. Each school day for two weeks I look through the window and dream of owning it. A week before Christmas, at the supper table my father asks if there's anything I'd like for Christmas. Immediately I think of the blue bicycle and quickly tell my parents about it. They listen but make no comment. Now when I walk by the cycle shop I find myself anxious, wondering if it's still there and hoping my parents will get it for me. One day after school, the bike is gone. I find myself torn between hope and disappointment. Christmas morning arrives and I rush downstairs. The bike is nowhere to be seen and I feel very disappointed. We all exchange gifts but the bike is not one of them. Mother has made a lovely breakfast and we sit around the table enjoying it but I feel crushed. After breakfast my father takes me out to the shed and there's the bicycle. Now I'm ecstatic.

Another scenario. I'm eighteen years old and I've played soccer since I could walk. My team is to play in the regional finals the next morning in a nearby park. I can hardly contain my excitement and have a hard time getting to sleep. At two in the morning I'm awakened by a loud rumbling sound that shakes my bed and, in fact, the whole house. I jump out of bed and run outside just in time to see the house come crashing down. All around me houses are similarly damaged. Throughout the night and the next day I work with others to help the injured and find the lost. I've no concern for the soccer game. It crosses my mind, but given the events around the earthquake, I know it's really of no importance.

One final scenario. I've fallen in love with a girl. I think the world of her but I know she's also dating another boy. After several months of this I find myself getting jealous and so one evening confront my girlfriend with an ultimatum. "Choose me or him. I'm not willing to share you with anyone else." She responds, "I'm sorry, but if I have to make a choice I'll choose him." I'm devastated, angry and depressed. My mind goes over the events like a dog worrying a bone. If I'd only been patient it might have been different. If I go and tell her she can date both of us maybe I can see her again. A year passes. One afternoon I'm at the beach reading. A shadow passes over my book and I look up to see a beautiful girl walk by. All the suffering of the past year has come to an end, and new suffering may be about to begin.

What, then is the common denominator in the four scenarios above? To give you an idea of what we're looking for, let me briefly describe three more separate events. A woman comes out of her second-floor apartment, trips on a piece of carpet and falls down the stairs. A man sits under an apple tree reading when an apple falls on his head. A man jumps out of an aircraft, pulls the ripcord and parachutes into a field.

What is the underlying common denominator in these events? It would have to be gravity, wouldn't it? Gravity operates the same way on all people and under all circumstances. If I step off a balcony and fall fifteen feet to the ground, breaking my leg, I can't blame gravity. And it doesn't matter whether I'm a nice person, a mean person, a black man or a white man, a man or a woman, an Englishman or a Canadian; gravity functions in the same impersonal manner with the same predictable results. To discover the source of all suffering we must look for the single underlying impersonal phenomenon that always operates with the same predictable results.

In the story of catching the plane, a number of events caused different degrees of suffering, all because expectations were not met. In the instance of the bike it's interesting to note that there was no suffering until the desire for the bike was voiced to my parents. At the age of nine there was already enough life experience to know that to desire something didn't guarantee the desire would be met. Because of the desire for the bike, however, there were several instances of suffering until my father took me out to the shed and showed me his gift. Then, in that moment all suffering concerning the bike came to an end. Why?

In the third scenario there was an expectation of playing soccer, which was for me an important event. The desire to play was there, and yet when the time came for the game to take place there was no upset, no suffering at all. Why?

It is reported that the Buddha said desire is the source of all suffering; and everyone knows that when we desire something, sometimes it will come to pass and sometimes it will not. Desire and expectation are important and natural in human attempts to bring about events, even changes in behavior. In other words, desire and expectations are motivational and natural, and by and large all human beings have them. What else, then, is the cause of suffering? What underlying aspect of life is it that functions in the same impersonal manner as does gravity, and with the same predictable results?

Attachment! It is our attachment to what we want. Attachment to desires and expectations is the single underlying source of all human suffering. I challenge you to find an exception!

In the first scenario of catching the plane, all the upset comes from attachment to the objects of desire, so not getting them creates suffering. In the second scenario, the moment I give voice to my desire in response to my father's question, I'm attached to the outcome. The minute I'm shown the bicycle on Christmas morning, there's no more suffering. Why? The attachment is gone; I now have what I once desired. In the third scenario the events surrounding the earthquake put my priorities into perspective, and as a result there's no attachment to playing the game. In this instance the detachment comes about simply because the events were so momentous as to preclude attachment. The attachment to the game has simply fallen away. It is worth noting that the absence of attachment enables one to engage in the selfless activity of trying to help those in need. In the fourth incident it is attachment to what I want with my girlfriend that creates the suffering. We have a saying, "Time heals all wounds." What this means is that with the passage of time attachment usually dissolves, and after a year or so the attachment is considerably weaker. Of course there are exceptions to this. There are some human beings who remain attached their whole lives and never know the peace that comes from detachment.

Attachment is not love

Attachment is often mistaken for love, but they are two very different things. When we examine attachment, it is what I want. It is inherently selfish. When I love, on the other hand, my actions and state of mind are unselfish. That is, what I want for you is what is best for you, whatever that might be. Let's say we've been married for a couple of years when you decide to go back to school. This entails you being away during the week and only home on weekends. I'm not happy with this because I want you home; I want to see you each day and sleep with you at night. I want you to cook for me and help with the chores around the home. I might even tell you this is because I love you and this is what loving couples do. But truthfully, is this love? No, it's not love, it's attachment. It's completely motivated from a selfish perspective. I'm more interested in me than you.

On the other hand, in loving you, I'm happy to have you go to school. I might miss your presence, your cooking, your smile and touch, but I'm more interested in what you want and how I can support you in accomplishing your objectives.

Much of what passes for love in our society is attachment. We can see this substitution in the lyrics of popular songs. It is particularly prevalent in country and western music. It's in our movies and plays as well and informs a great deal of what we expect in marriage. This makes life difficult for the young, as they have few models to go by.

When a man knows the harmony and vitality of a child
It is a great gift.
When permanent
It is enlightenment.

Lao Tzu

Chapter 6
Enlightenment

Crisis

For most human beings there appears to be a kind of hunger, the vague sense of looking for something, that something is missing or an expectation that things will be better in the future. What do we think we're missing? Several words point to it—success, happiness, peace of mind. In one way or another we come to believe that we can achieve what we're missing through acquiring power, prestige and possessions; in fact, that's what our culture teaches us. If we can obtain all three, power, prestige and possessions, so much the better; but even one by itself is better than none at all. What we find, however, is the opposite; the peace of mind we'd hoped for is not attainable. By and large, the more wealth we obtain, the more anxious we are to hold on to it, protect it and invest it. The more power we have, the more miserable we become; and the more prestige we have, the more concerned we are about what others think of us.

Though life is generally far from peaceful, there are always a small percentage of people with great wealth who've also found peace of mind—not because of their wealth, but in spite of it. The same thing can be said for the acquisition of power and prestige. Usually they do not bring what we're looking for but rather the opposite.

At times in life we may experience a crisis of some kind. It could take the form of a bankruptcy, loss of one's job, loss of one's marriage, loss of one's health, death of a loved one, or war; or it could even come from an apparently "positive" event, a success, or retirement. At such times we may realize that what we sought in the outer world did not bring us what we'd hoped for. Achievement in the outer world is not designed to bring us the underlying peace of mind we seek; but we must come to understand this from personal experience.

At this point there may be a turning within. Perhaps, we think, what we're looking for can be found inside ourselves. Sometimes the turning inward springs from a deep desire to understand ourselves, while at other times it is an exploration of religion, belief systems, scripture and religious doctrine. Some may engage in spiritual practices of one kind or another—meditation, contemplation, yoga, prayer, japa, the reciting of a mantra and so on. This could be called the beginning of the spiritual search. Something present in us since early in life begins to burn with considerable intensity.

There are those who in turning to religion become what can be called true believers. They've settled for belief—the menu, not the meal; for some this is where the search ends. Those who move beyond belief are often dislodged by another crisis, what might be called a crisis of faith. Many religious organizations have an image of what is considered a person of faith. Within the Christian tradition one idea has been the "imitation of Christ." But it is not possible to imitate Christ, or any master, for that matter. What the master has is not an imitation of anything; it is real, it's at the root of things, and what he says and how he lives is simply an original expression of a profound understanding known as enlightenment. Consequently all attempts to imitate the master are bound to fail. We are not capable of living in the way we've come to believe we should. We are incapable of meeting our own expectations; there's a disturbing discrepancy between what we believe and what we practice. This is known as hypocrisy. Given the nature of the ego, it is not easy to become aware of this discrepancy, however. The ego loves images and portrays itself as a good Christian, a good Jew or Muslim—in short, a Godly person, an image it is reluctant to give up. Thus it does not generally recognize hypocrisy. To become aware of it requires an interest in truth that supersedes everything else.

• • • What is enlightenment?

There are a number of definitions for enlightenment, but the one used throughout this book is as follows. Enlightenment is the permanent dissolution of the individualized consciousness referred to as the ego, the identified consciousness. With the dissolution of the ego there's a recovery of the original, impersonal consciousness of birth.

Christ referred to this in several ways; first by stating, in more general terms, that one could not enter the kingdom of heaven except by becoming as a little child. The kingdom of heaven, of course, is enlightenment, and the consciousness of a little child is the impersonal consciousness, prior to the development of the ego. In the gospel of John he also went on to say, "I am the way, the truth and the light, no man cometh unto the Father but by me." What is meant in this very clear statement is this. The I am, the sense of presence, the impersonal consciousness, free of the ego, is what is real; it is the light, consciousness itself; and no man can come to the Father (another name for God or enlightenment) except through the sense of presence, the I am—which, to reiterate, is free of the ego. In the Hindu tradition Brahman and Atman are of the same essence. Atman is the impersonal consciousness and Brahman the Totality of Consciousness.

Does this mean that the sense of identification with the name and form is suddenly gone? No. If someone called the Buddha by name he would have responded. The deep identification with the ego, however, does not exist.

What is to be understood?

If we look up the definition of the word "identity," we'll discover something along these lines: that which is identified stands out or stands apart from the background or foreground of something; that which is identified is separate from the whole. The personal consciousness is the identified consciousness and comprises the individual's identity, who or what he considers himself to be; and it is this that stands out from the impersonal consciousness.

This distinction is important. In both philosophy and theology there is a definition that says God is everywhere at all times, all-powerful and all-knowing. If that is the case, then it follows that there's nothing that is not God, including us. If someone said, "I want to see God," I would tell them to look around, and whatever they saw would have to be part of the body of God, so to speak. If God is everywhere present, all knowing and all-powerful, then I would also have to be God. But, when I honestly examine my experience I would have to say I don't know this. I might believe it, but I'm no longer interested in menus. So, why then do I have no awareness of this? The word "identity" provides the clue. My personal consciousness is the identified consciousness, and as such it naturally stands apart from the whole. With this comes the understanding that the only way the human being can ever directly know or be one with God, is for the ego, the identity, the separate sense of consciousness, to fade away.

Once the spiritual seeker understands this on an intellectual level, it may bring a certain sense of peacefulness, a sense of relief.

Look for It and It cannot be seen
Listen for It and It cannot be heard
Reach for It and It slips through the fingers.

Above It there's no brightness
Below It no darkness
Seamless and unnamed
It is the ever pregnant silence.

Formless Itself
It holds all forms.
Though concepts point to It
It is beyond all concepts.

Approach It and there is no beginning
Follow It and there is no end

It can never be known
For what It is
We already are.

This is wisdom!

Lao Tzu

Chapter 7
"The Way"

The gradual approach

There are two basic approaches to spiritual awakening, the gradual approach and the direct approach. The gradual approach involves spiritual practice and spiritual discipline. From this perspective practice brings the student to different levels of understanding, even what are considered different levels of enlightenment. The goal, however, is full awakening, full enlightenment.

Some examples of this approach are as follows. In meditation the student may be instructed to concentrate on his breath to the exclusion of all else. To begin with, the student finds himself distracted by sounds, such as a baby crying or a dog barking.

Sometimes he's distracted by his back aching, his legs going to sleep, or his nose itching. At other times he may find himself thinking about something that happened earlier or something he hopes or fears might happen. In all these situations he'll find himself incapable of following the inhalation and exhalation of his breath. Over many years of practice he may eventually develop a certain level of control. This is a major accomplishment.

Another practice could be to repeat a mantra, recite the rosary, repeat prayers, spin prayer wheels, or make a mandala. For these practices to be alive and vibrant, they cannot be a matter of mere repetition. Such practices take a great deal of discipline and long periods of time; ten, twenty years or more is not uncommon. Once more this is a major accomplishment.

But for whom is this an accomplishment? Is it not an accomplishment for the ego? In conversation with such disciplined spiritual seekers it is not uncommon for them to compare notes. "What kind of meditation do you practice?" "Oh, I see. I do Vipassana Meditation myself, twice a day." "You meditate for how long? Eight hours a day? Well, I meditate six hours in the morning, take a meal break, do a walking meditation and then back for another six hours." How do such seekers find time to live their lives? But that's not the point. What is going on here is comparing and judging. The ego is back in full force; in fact it never really went away. This practitioner's syndrome is what the Tibetan Rinpoche

Chogyam Trungpa called “spiritual materialism.”

The accomplishments are accomplishments of the ego. Just as the ego was involved in the accomplishments of the outer world, so the ego is involved in the accomplishments of the inner world.

Ramesh was often asked about meditation, was it something that should be practiced by the spiritual seeker? His response was always the same. If you’re using meditation as a tool to become enlightened, don’t bother. If on the other hand you find yourself falling naturally into a meditative state, that is fine; enjoy it, allow it to happen as often as it occurs, but don’t turn it into a practice.

The story is told of Buddhist nuns who, as part of their ritual, lit candles in front of small personal statues of the Buddha. The statues were kept on a side altar in the temple. One particularly devout nun arranged to have her Buddha made from white marble. Compared to the other statues he was the most beautiful of them all. One evening while lighting the candle she noticed her statue reflected light, which illuminated the statues next to it. To prevent this she fashioned a funnel which she placed upside down over her candle so that the light shone only on the beautiful face of her Buddha and not on the other Buddhas. In the morning when she went and checked on her Buddha she found his face was now completely covered in soot.

••• Three yogas

Loosely speaking, the term yoga means "path." In India, although there are many different forms of yoga, there are three main ones: Bhakti, Karma, and Jnanna (pronounced "Yana"). For those who seek the ultimate understanding, the question arises, "What path should I take?" I would suggest that we do not choose the path, for in a sense the path chooses us. Our temperament determines the path most conducive to it; that is, specific paths appeal to specific people. One path is more appealing to the kind of person we are than another.

Earlier, certain aspects of the gradual approach were described. Bhakti and Karma Yoga fall into this category. Jnanna Yoga is known as the direct approach and this will be explained later.

Bhakti attracts people who are more devotional in their approach. Such people are drawn to spiritual practice and can be fairly disciplined. At a certain point the need arises for someone who can help guide and give them instruction. They'll be drawn to someone who can help them—a guru. They will deeply appreciate his loving guidance and in some cases may even fall in love with him. In Irena Tweedy's book *Chasm of Fire*, she describes her relationship with her guru, a Sufi master. The master taught her various spiritual practices and presided over them. She thought she was in love with him. At first he gave her unqualified access but slowly became less and less available to her. In this way he taught her that this love was in fact attachment. It took her a long time to realize what he was doing, and she suffered a great deal. He was eventually able to show her that love for the guru had to be transformed to love for God. Finally, to love God completely the ego and the concept of God would have to dissolve.

There's a saying in Buddhism, "When you meet the Buddha on the road, kill him." What this means is that for the seeker to worship the master is a trap. Once the seeker realizes this, once the seeker wakes up, he no longer worships the Buddha. The Buddha for him is dead. Buddha nature is alive and well, and does not exist just within the Buddha. In the moment of awakening, the Buddha and the disciple are one and the same, although occupying different bodies.

Karma Yoga is known as the yoga of action. Those attracted to this path are those who like to take action, those who like to serve, those who have a strong desire to be of assistance and to ease suffering. Such people will often be found in the healing professions. At first they'll do what they do for pay or for a reward. For some, their giving or service is acknowledged by having their name inscribed on a park bench. Sometimes a philanthropist will donate money for a hospital or hospital wing, and in the entrance to the hospital a large painting of him will hang, along with words of appreciation. At some point someone who is a natural Karma yogi will come to realize that he serves because of the deep satisfaction he finds in service. As this realization sinks in, his giving and service become selfless; he no longer has the need to be recognized or acknowledged, because the ego has died. Mother Teresa was a good example of a Karma yogi.

There is a delightful story of a Zen master who wanted to introduce his disciples to the idea of selfless service. He did this in a very ingenious way. He told the monks to come to the main hall of the temple before going to supper. When they arrived there were a large number of wooden boards and a quantity of rope cut into two-foot lengths. The master took the boards and tied them to the arms of each of his students in such a way as to prevent them from bending their elbows. Then he sent them to the dining hall for supper. When the master entered the monks were seated in their accustomed positions facing each other across tables, which stretched the length of the hall. After the master gave a brief reading, the food was ladled into the bowls before them. Then the master watched.

At first there was consternation amongst the monks as they tried to bring the spoons of food to their mouths. Not being able to bend their elbows, they found it impossible. Then, after a few moments one of the monks took his spoonful of food and offered it to his brother monk sitting across from him. In moments all the monks were enjoying their meal.

I lived for many years in Hawaii. During that time I had a private counseling practice. As part of my work

I took family cases referred to me by Child Protective Services. At times the families with whom I worked were poor, sometimes not having adequate furniture, bedding, or refrigeration. In the village where I lived there was a grocery store. The family that ran the store was deeply caring, friendly and outgoing. The father, I knew, was a Buddhist. One day I approached him and asked if he could help. The family I was working with had no beds for their children. He took me outside and we talked. He said he would help and was glad to do so. He had one provision, however. Under no circumstances was I to reveal his name to anyone concerning what he'd done. Over the years I had occasion to seek his help, which he granted freely and with quiet joy. Never once did I reveal his name, as I respected his wish to be anonymous. In Karma Yoga the end result is the same as Bhakti Yoga: the dissolution of the ego.

The direct approach

Jnanna Yoga is known as the direct approach. It begins, in a sense, where the other yogas end. It recognizes that the ego is the only obstacle to awakening. Jnanna Yoga attracts those with keen intellects who are philosophically inclined. It is simple and direct and points to the obvious. There are no spiritual practices to be engaged in, as it recognizes that only the ego engages in such things and thus takes pride in its accomplishments. Jnanna Yoga is the path of wisdom and direct understanding, and those who find themselves attracted to it are, by and large, those who've found the other paths not to their liking. Of course, none of the paths are completely isolated from one another. Those attracted to the path of Jnanna often blend with Karma Yoga; and when it comes to the guru, there can be a very strong emotional connection as well, similar to the guru-disciple relationship found in Bhakti. In this instance, however, the love for the guru is born of a deep appreciation for what the guru has helped the disciple understand. Throughout this book, what is being described is, in fact, Jnanna Yoga as found in Taoism, Advaita Vedanta and Zen.

The trap of hubris

The problem with hypocrisy was mentioned earlier, and the fact that the ego can never acknowledge hypocrisy was pointed out. The ego always finds a way to rationalize what it does and to avoid the use of such a term—except of course, when it perceives it in someone else. This is *the* most serious danger for the spiritual seeker in the awakening process.

In esoteric Christianity there are two terms that point to this trap. One is called the "Sin against the Holy Spirit," and the other is known as the "Unforgivable Sin." What these terms refer to is the same thing. Let me share from my own experience something that illustrates the danger for the spiritual seeker.

I met a man, an illiterate Scottish welder named Sid.

The year before meeting him, a spontaneous awakening had taken place while I was pondering the issue of suffering and the nature of perfection. At the time I had a deep awareness that life was eternal; there was no place to go, and nothing to achieve; life was perfect as it was. This was accompanied by a timeless awareness that I had always been and always would be. I also had the strange ability to know things before they happened. I could see into people, so to speak, and see clearly the source of their disturbance. I did not sleep for several days. The psychic abilities continued for many months following the initial experience.

At the time, I was teaching courses for members of the two rural parishes where I served as a minister. I hoped to share with them what I'd discovered. There were a number of parishioners who, like me, were deeply interested in spiritual matters, beyond the formalities of organized religion. I've also enjoyed teaching too, using spontaneous and interactive conversation and dialogue, coupled with teaching stories from the Sufi, Zen, Taoist and Christian traditions. The courses I taught at the time spanned a period of twelve months. One day I realized that what I'd known on a deep and intimate level, the eternalness of my nature, was no longer alive in me—it was now delivered from memory, second-hand, as it were.

I met Sid for the first time at his home. The couple who introduced us were parishioners with whom

I'd been doing marriage counseling. At one point, Sid looked at me and started to tell me things about myself, my state of mind, things that no one but I could know, or so I thought. I was shocked and frightened by the experience. The fear was of being exposed, that somehow he'd seen some unforeseen hypocrisy in my life. In good psychological fashion I told him not to make assumptions about me and that if he wanted to talk about such things perhaps he should speak from his own experience and not presume to know what was so for me. He looked at me with a smile and said that he was not speaking from assumptions but from what he saw to be fact. I became angry with him: Who did he think he was? In that moment I realized that my reaction was one aspect of what he was talking about, that he had indeed accurately assessed me. I shut up at once, not wishing to be exposed any further, and insisted that I would speak for myself and he should speak only for himself. He saw the ploy, smiled and said nothing.

Sid turned his attention to the couple and began to describe what he saw about them and their relationship; things I also knew to be true, things I'd been trying to help them with. I watched and listened and could see that they were using the same technique I'd used, in order not to hear what he had to say. Realizing the opportunity before them, I waited for a break in the conversation. Then I told the couple that what Sid had told me about myself was indeed true. I didn't know how he could so accurately assess me, but he had. I then told them that what he had been seeing in them was also what I had noticed and had tried to show them. They got it at once. Sid was impressed.

I later learned that Sid had suddenly, spontaneously awakened nine months before, and since that time a small group of followers had gathered around him. Sometime after that he came to teach in the town where I lived and stopped by to say hello. He brought a beautiful handmade candle. He said how impressed he was with me in our last conversation, and that what I'd done had taken a lot of courage. Once more, I found myself turned off by his comments. Who did he think he was?

Later in the year I was teaching in the town where he lived. I didn't see it at the time but somehow I'd set myself up in competition with him. More people came to see me than to see him. After all, I was an eloquent, educated university graduate, and Sid, an illiterate welder working at the local mill.

My wife and I went to see Sid several times on the island where he'd eventually settled. I found myself put off by what I took as the fawning attitude of his followers; I was not impressed with gurus, although I barely knew what the term meant.

Six months later I received a tape recording from Sid. In it he said, "You have refused to acknowledge me as the source of your inspiration and in so doing have denied God." With a pounding headache I taped a response stating categorically that what he said was not true. Technically, that is, what he said was not true—he was not the source of my inspiration—but I understood his point. Sid had once more seen through me. We always know the truth; we recognize it as being so. I also said that the ego could never admit to being hypocritical, as it always has an inflated image of itself. When I received the tape from Sid I recognized the truth at some level, but quickly the ego asserted itself and I sent out the rebuttal tape.

Through most of my life I have felt relatively at peace in the world. The Christian idea of sin had minimal effect on my life before I rejected it out of hand. I was a child of the universe and thus a child of the Creator, and the whole concept of sin, salvation, heaven and hell were preposterous concepts. I could not accept them. Since meeting Sid, however, I was feeling alienated from the very universe that brought me forth. A question arose in the mind. "Why had God turned his face from me?" There was no answer, and slowly despair seeped into every aspect of my life.

I found myself thinking about the sin against the Holy Spirit again, the unforgivable sin. The question persisted for months. I wondered; is there anything that might happen that I could not find in my heart to forgive? Thinking about this, I came to realize there was nothing that had happened or might happen that I was incapable of forgiving. Understanding this led me to conclude that whatever this concept of God represented, God would have to be at least as forgiving as me; he certainly couldn't be any less. Following this reasoning, it was clear that the unforgivable sin was brought about by man himself, and not by any willful behavior on God's part. Could there be a blindness in man, a blindness about which he was deeply unaware, a blindness that kept him lost and removed from the Source? Suddenly the word "hubris" came to mind. The definition of hubris is "overweening pride." To believe one understands, when understanding has not taken place, blocks the seeker from seeing the problem. It is arrogance that blinds us from seeing the truth about ourselves and it is precisely this arrogance that provides the trap. The arrogance is nothing other than the ego. The blind arrogance of ego leaves us in the wilderness and gives rise to the sensation that God has turned his face from us.

Whatever is destined not to happen
Will not happen, try as you might.
Whatever is destined to happen will happen,
Do what you may to prevent it.
This is certain.
The best course, therefore,
Is to remain silent.
Ramana Maharshi

Chapter 8
Free Will

The illusion

If it is accepted that the ego is the obstacle to the goal of the spiritual seeker, then it follows that the spiritual seeker would be well served to be rid of the ego. But can he get rid of it? The apostle Paul said something along these lines: "What I do, I would rather not do, and what I would do, I do not." All of us have had this experience and it goes to the heart of the issue of free will.

We are taught in life that we have free will, that it is our birthright, something of the utmost importance, something that sets us apart from all other animals. It is perhaps the most cherished belief in Western cultures. It is, however, an assumption, an assumption rarely challenged and even more rarely examined with rigor. This belief is a cornerstone of the ego's fantasy. Its inability to see reality is a natural and inevitable consequence of the process of endarkenment.

What is the definition of free will? Most definitions fall along the following lines. "Freedom of self-determination and action, independent of external causes." "The power of making free choices that are unconstrained by external circumstances or by an agency such as fate or divine will." Think about it. *Freedom to have our actions determined by ourselves without the influence of any external causes.* What such a definition suggests is that I should be able to choose something and obtain the result I'm looking for, and to do so without the influence of anything outside myself. This raises the issue as to who or what it is that constitutes the me who operates freely and independently—but more on that shortly. Essentially the definition suggests that I should be able to freely choose something, so let's begin there.

What color do you like and what color do you not like? Let's say the color you like is blue and the color you dislike is red. First of all, can you help liking what you like and disliking what you dislike? If you have free will you should be able to exchange your likes and dislikes. That being the case, I want you to like red and dislike blue and to do so honestly. Can you do it; can you genuinely like something you genuinely dislike; can you genuinely dislike something you genuinely like? It can't be done, can it?

Let's examine this issue more closely. Take for instance the precursor to this book—how did it come about? Without going back to the beginning of time, let's simply start when I took a trip to Victoria. It was a sunny and brisk day in May when I found myself walking into a book store. Upon entering I happened to notice a large display of books, and one book in particular caught my eye. It was a new book by an author with whom I was familiar, someone quite popular as a spiritual teacher. I picked up the book and leafed through it. The book was a guide for spiritual seekers and what they must do to progress along the spiritual path. In reading I found myself thinking, "Why make it so complex, when it is so simple?"

When I got back to the hotel I picked up pen and paper and in a few minutes jotted down a number of points I thought important to the spiritual process. I carried the notes over the next few days and added to them as certain points came to mind. When I got home I sat down at the computer and the writing flowed effortlessly. Although busy with other things I found myself looking forward to writing. By the end of two weeks a large portion of the book was done and within six weeks it was completed.

Now, such events as those described are usually attributed to free will, but where did I make a choice in the matter? I happened to be in Victoria, I happened to go into the bookstore and saw the book. In reading it I had a reaction to it, over which I had no control. My experience as a seeker played a role too, and over that I had no choice either. It was important for me to get accurate information with which to examine life more closely.

When we examine our actions we find a set of events taking place. Thoughts enter the mind, appearing to come from nowhere, and create a number of responses: either taking action, going in a particular direction, or preventing action. Outside circumstances take place too—unexpected events, phone calls, letters, people showing up, seeing a book, overhearing a portion of conversation, a headline in the paper, an ad on the bus—and all of these things impinge on the process. When we reduce it to the bare essentials, what is happening? We move between the poles of attraction and repulsion; and what results, we consider our action, the exercise of our free will.

Someone reading this book, a spiritual seeker for instance, with a strong ego, may find himself reacting negatively to the idea of not having free will. Perhaps he might try a little experiment. If he does indeed have free will, then he should be able to change his negative reaction to a positive one, and to do so genuinely.

To understand this process it is important that we do our own investigation. For instance one might, in the evening, look back over the day's events to see if we can follow what happened. See if we can identify the contributing stimuli—thoughts, events, people, circumstances, and so on; all those things that brought forth the particular actions, non-actions, and changes in direction. As we examine them we must answer the question: Did they simply happen as a result of our uninfluenced choices or were they derived from factors beyond our control?

Consider the following. A man goes to the store to pick up, amongst other things, razor blades. There are two ways to go and he decides to take the longer way as it's more scenic. When the car starts the radio comes on and he finds himself listening to a favorite program. Engrossed in the program, he inadvertently takes the wrong turn, taking instead the shorter route, not the one originally intended. Arriving at the store, he buys the things needed for the house and leaves. He remembers to drop off some DVDs for a friend. On the way he suddenly remembers the razor blades. The program he's listening to is so interesting he decides to continue home. He takes the long way, enjoying the budding trees, the crocuses, daffodils and snow drops, and of course, the program. A thought in the mind provides some comfort: he doesn't really need the razor blades at the moment; he can get by.

When we examine the events in our own lives we can't help but notice the same process taking place. It's these events and our reactions that we claim as our own and therefore as proof of our free will! But, is it really our will and is it really free, free of any outside input? Definitions of free will suggest that external stimuli also include thoughts that suddenly appear in the mind. But our so-called free will, given the reality of our daily lives, does not meet the definition.

If we have free will, should we not be able to take action and obtain the intended result? If not, what value is there to this free will of ours? Do our actions bring about the intended results? We would have to conclude that some of the time we get the intended results and some of the time we don't. How then, do we explain this inconsistency and still maintain a belief in free will?

If the results do not match our intentions, we explain it in one of several ways. "It's his fault it didn't work," or, "Circumstances beyond our control interfered," or, "We simply lacked the discipline necessary," or, "We really didn't want it anyway." What about those things that do work according to our intention? Of course, we think, *I* did it, *I* was successful, no doubt about it! But when we examine what took place, there are all manner of events and circumstances that simply happened, events and thoughts that came from outside and were certainly beyond our control. If we are dispassionate in the examination of the facts, we would have to conclude we had little effect on the results, other than the fact that we were one of a number of instruments through which a result took place.

I went to see Ramesh a couple of years before his

death. He had changed his approach to the issue of free will. "Yes," he would say, "You do have free will; you can choose whatever you wish, but will it always give you what you hoped it would? If your free will does not always give you what you want when making your choice, of what use is it?" To drive the point home he told the following story. "A person is given a million dollars, a million real dollars; fives, tens, twenties, fifties, hundreds. But, he can't spend it, no one will take it. Does he have a million dollars? Yes, he does. The only problem is that the money was old and taken out of circulation, retired from active duty, so to speak, and it is worthless."

The ego always takes credit for getting what it wants, and always blames others, events, or its own lack of discipline for its failures. It is this behavior, this rationalization, that maintains the myth of free will.

Personally, I'd been a firm believer in free will. It gave me a sense of pride in the things I'd done and what I thought of as hope for the future. It gave me a sense of freedom. The idea was intoxicating. I thought I could do anything. I went into pre-med, having *chosen* to be a doctor. But the love of literature and philosophy trumped all effort to succeed in physics, calculus and biology. It was obvious to me that I lacked will power. If I applied myself to those studies instead of entertaining myself at night with reading the novels of Dostoevsky, the poems of Wordsworth and T. S. Elliot, the life of Socrates and the thinking of Spinoza and Plotinus, perhaps I would get more sleep and I would be less tired for those dreaded calculus exams. At the end of the first year I was in deep trouble. My advisor administered an aptitude and interest test. Philosophy and literature were two of the main fields where aptitude and interest strongly coincided. I dropped out of pre-med and it was as if the wind was at my back and the sails were full. Now I could pursue my two major loves without guilt. When the change was made I felt immediate relief, a sense of fullness and well-being that, in a manner of speaking, came from the heart. I was now free to do what came naturally. Enrollment in pre-med was one of the few times I chose with my mind. Before and since that time I have always followed my heart.

So despite my belief in free will, it seems direction always came from the heart, and the proper relationship of the mind to the heart was, in fact, as servant; not the other way round. But we are not in control of either the impulses of the heart or the mind. By the time I met Ramesh it didn't take much to undermine this already shaky edifice. The belief in free will was terminated quickly although it took some time to realize what had happened.

What finally put an end to the matter was something that came from a direction I'd not anticipated—from the question, what is it that I am, what is this me I take myself to be, who am I?

The illusory self

We've spoken earlier about the formation of the ego, but really, what is it? As was mentioned, the only thing I know for sure is that I exist, that I am. I am, the sense of presence, is quite different from the concept of "I am David or Joan" with all its attendant stories. The personal consciousness, the ego, as was pointed out, is not primary; it derives its existence, such as it is, from the impersonal consciousness. Another metaphor might be helpful here. When we look at a shadow cast by a pole in the ground, the shadow is real but is dependent for its existence on sunlight. In order for the shadow to exist, light must first exist. Light would be considered primary, the pole secondary, and the shadow, the consequence of the other two.

When we examine the idea of the ego we have to acknowledge that it is in fact an idea, a concept, something suggested by Freud as part of his explanation of the human personality and behavior derived from it. The ego then is simply an inference, a concept that points to something that has never been seen, located, touched, or heard.

The sailor pays attention to the water, looking for the patterns, the ruffles, the disturbances that suggest where the wind can be found to fill the sails. From the disturbances on the water it can be inferred that wind is present. It would seem that the ego functions in much the same way. That is, it loves disturbance and through attachment finds itself constantly upset over life. This disturbance suggests by inference there is "someone" who exists to be happy or unhappy. What happens with awakening, however, is that the ego dies, and when that takes place life is taken as it comes; there's no suffering because there's no attachment, and life is experienced in the present moment, with no references from the mind concerning the past and the future. As a result there is no disturbance that suggests the presence of "someone," of the ego. What remains is the impersonal consciousness with which we were born.

The implications of this realization are considerable; and it was one implication, in particular, that put an end to my mind's insistence on free will. If there really is no me, if the ego is simply a concept, then it would have to follow that there's no "one" to have free will. Think about it. If what I've taken myself to be—the ego, the personal consciousness with all its attendant stories, the me—is simply a concept and not real, then who is there to have free will?

Why is a concept not real? The concept that comprises the personal consciousness, as was mentioned earlier, is dependent for its very existence upon the impersonal consciousness with which we are born. When we compare the sense of I am (the impersonal presence) to the me (the ego, the story, the personal sense of being), we are forced to conclude that only the I am is real. This conclusion becomes obvious when we consider those who've lost their memories. Until the ego develops again, what is present is simply the impersonal consciousness, free of all personal history.

The stories and concepts that comprise the personal consciousness are real stories, and real concepts, but they lack the immediacy, the unassailable reality of the impersonal awareness, the sense of I am. Furthermore, the concepts we hold of ourselves, along with our personal story, change over time and differ from person to person. The impersonal awareness of existence, however, does not change and is, in fact, the same in all human beings, although the content of consciousness differs from person to person.

A friend wrote the following letter.

Free Will—truth or dogma?

I found the concept of not having free will a difficult one. It felt as if everything I had achieved in life had somehow been defiled. All the good things I had done—which I remembered not with pride but with quiet satisfaction—and all the kindnesses I had shown, suddenly meant nothing. And what of the decisions I had struggled with endlessly before coming to a conclusion? To think that none of this was under my control made me angry, at least to begin with. It left me with a sense of powerlessness. I thought I had been driving the car all these years, only to find I was just a passenger.

Life gets very complicated at times, and I think the most important thing is to keep one's mind open and try to see what is fact and what is judgment and belief. When I looked closely at my life I could see that decisions were being made by my character, my personality, which reacted to outside circumstances and to thoughts in my mind. And over none of this did I have any control. In looking closer it became clear that I had no choice as to my character, either. I sometimes wish I had.

It took about a year to strip away judgement and belief and see what was actually happening in my life.

Here are some things that helped me. All decisions are made as a result of thoughts. Thoughts simply arise and it is clear we have no control over them—as in the story about a Zen master telling his students that under no circumstances are they to think of monkeys. From personal experience it is clear I have no control over my thoughts. My actions are a result of many things: thoughts, emotions, circumstances, genetic makeup, conditioning and so on, over all of which I have absolutely no control. So given all these factors, where does free will leap in to help make a decision?

As the idea of free will begins to dissolve, there's a great feeling of freedom and even some peace in the acceptance that free will is just a belief. If I'm not the doer, the author of my actions, it's not my fault, so I don't judge myself (much). The main freedom lies in not judging others. Knowing they can't help themselves brings freedom from blame and acceptance that what happens, happens. Life simply is, as it is.

Not having free will doesn't appear to affect my sense of responsibility. I still do the best I can to make decisions. It's just that when they turn out wrong I don't feel so much guilt, and when they turn out right I don't feel any pride.

I've noticed that some people get very angry when it is suggested they have no free will. They argue that we have to take responsibility for our actions. From my point of view I still act according to my character and programming. Whether I accept responsibility or not is irrelevant. I react as I've learned to react to circumstances which arise. So since I now know I have no responsibility, what can I do with this new freedom? Nothing. I can't act outside my character. Responsibility is just another word—another concept to block a view to the truth.

None of this is about dogma for me—it is simply about trying to understand myself. I believed I had free will and it took deep searching of events in my life and how I reacted to them, to realize the control I valued so highly was just a belief. It was thinking I had control over my life that turned out to be dogma.

Something I've noticed; the intellectual understanding of such things, may not be enlightenment, but it brings a measure of peace, with less and less tendency to take offence, and for that I am deeply grateful.

• • • In conclusion

What, then, is the end result of this examination? Would we not have to conclude that the idea of free will is a myth, simply a belief system? And, would we not also have to conclude that the personal self, that which we've taken ourselves for, is also a myth, a belief system?

The ego, being what it is, is not easily overcome, and the whole edifice around it is not readily yielded. But this thorough examination may crack the absolute certainty of our cultural assumptions on the topic. If this happens then our life experiences provide the irrefutable evidence that will in time complete the process.

The problem for the ego is that the good news is bad news.

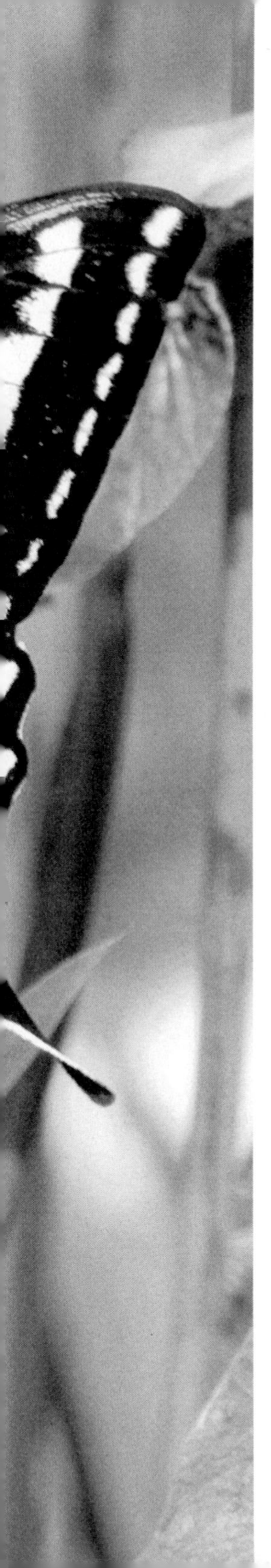

Chapter 9
Bad News, Good News

The bad news

For spiritual seekers, the realization that we have no free will can come as a shock. When coupled with the fact that who we've taken ourselves to be, the ego, isn't real either, it is a major blow. For close to thirty years I was consumed with the desire for enlightenment; it superseded everything else in my life. It was "the pearl of great price" and I wanted it more than anything else. Enlightenment was the last thought when falling asleep at night and the first thought upon awakening. I voraciously read everything I could get my hands on. The end result was a deep exploration of a number of spiritual traditions. I believed I could bring about enlightenment if I were disciplined, but by nature I was not disciplined. I didn't believe in gurus either. It seemed obvious to me that each person must learn to swim for himself. But I was desperate; I needed to find someone who "knew," someone who was enlightened, someone I hoped could answer my questions.

In January 1990 I found myself at the ashram of Sai Baba in Puttapharti. I looked into Sai Baba's eyes and knew he was not the person I'd been looking for. The trip to India did, however, prove fruitful. In the city of Bangalore, the night before leaving for Puttapharti, I came across the teachings of the recently deceased Advaita master, Nisargadatta Maharaj. In reading his book I knew immediately that what he spoke was the truth. Upon my return to Hawaii I reread the book, deeply fascinated by what he had to say. As it turned out, he had an enlightened disciple by the name of Ramesh S. Balsekar whose work I began to read next. In the autumn of 1990 I flew to Hermosa Beach where he was speaking.

At the first meeting I had the opportunity to speak with Ramesh and ask questions. A diminutive man, mild and soft-spoken but exceptionally well versed in both science and philosophy, Ramesh attracted me at a very deep level, far deeper than I realized at the time. In response to a question he said, "The seeker is the obstacle to that which is sought." In that moment it was as if I had stepped off a cliff. In that moment the intense thirty-year search came to a sudden end. I fully understood that I could do absolutely nothing to bring about the enlightenment I so desperately desired. I further realized that all effort to use spiritual practice and spiritual discipline to achieve enlightenment would be futile, since what was seeking enlightenment was the ego, the very thing that prevented enlightenment from happening in the first place. The ego's attempts to become enlightened were as futile as running to reach the horizon.

In that brief moment the sole purpose of my life had been brushed away. Suddenly life had no meaning. As the days passed into months everything seemed flat, devoid of emotion. The excitement and sense of wild anticipation that had filled my life during the search had vanished. I found myself in a world that seemed peculiarly tasteless.

Around the time I met Ramesh I also met the French Advaita master, Dr. Jean Klein. As with Ramesh, I recognized that what he had to say was the truth. Three months after my conversation with Ramesh I flew from Hawaii to New York. One evening I went to see Dr. Klein, who happened to be speaking in the basement of a Unitarian Church. As I sat in the front row and listened I had the strangest experience. As he spoke, my mind registered the words before he uttered them. This went on for perhaps twenty minutes. It was as if I was perfectly attuned to the source of his words. At one point he stopped and, looking directly at me, smiled. Somehow I think he was aware of what had happened.

I made an appointment to see him the next day. He was staying near Central Park. When I arrived he ushered me into a warm cozy room with wood-paneled walls, antique furniture and beautiful rugs. Dr. Klein scuffed around in a pair of old worn slippers, which didn't fit my image of this well-dressed European gentleman with whom I was familiar from attending several of his public talks in Seattle. We sat across from one another while outside, a cold blustery winter wind rattled the windows. "What is your question?" he asked. I told him life had suddenly become flat and meaningless; that the joy had gone out of it. He asked me what had happened. I found myself recounting the experience of the meeting with Ramesh, and the statement, "The seeker is the obstacle to that which is sought." Dr. Klein paused for a moment and then with a voice that seemed to hiss he said: "And, you know, of course, the seeker *is* the sought." He watched me closely for a moment before asking me to describe the flatness. I told him it was a kind of mild depression, that life seemed emotionally flat and tasteless. Fixing me with eyes that peered from under untamed bushy eyebrows, he said, "Refuse to name it; live with the experience without naming, and let it yield itself to you."

When I left the apartment the wind was gusting and leaves twirled on unseen currents, the sun was setting and it was cold. Christmas was not far away. As I walked along the sidewalk, the grocery stalls outside the little stores were flooded with people selecting fresh vegetables for supper on their way home from work. Buses appeared and just as urgently left, disgorging passengers at each stop. Suddenly I heard one of the most haunting sounds I had ever heard. The sound of a single violin—part gypsy, part cosmic blues; it felt like the soul's longing to be home in this unfathomable universe.

Walking toward the sound, I came upon a middle-aged man dressed in a long woolen overcoat, dark pants with sharply pressed creases, and black highly polished dress shoes. His hands were encased in grey woolen gloves with the fingers cut out, and on his head he wore a smart matching fedora. He was playing the most beautiful rendition of Christmas carols I'd ever heard. People had gathered around, equally enthralled. A young woman came down the sidewalk pushing a stroller with her toddler muffled against the cold. Lost in thought, she'd not noticed the music or musician. The little boy had. As she pushed the child through the open space in front of the musician the child's eyes were locked on the violinist and his little body twisted hard to see him as he went by. The young mother suddenly realized what was happening, turned the stroller to face the violinist, and she too became absorbed in the music. Reaching down she kissed her son on the cheek, and in doing so revealed a long slender neck. I looked at the violinist and he at me and both of us smiled at the beauty of that gentle event. That memory has always been indelibly linked to the meeting with Dr. Klein.

I did as Dr. Klein suggested, and even though the emptiness continued for another year, I eventually forgot about it; perhaps I'd become accustomed to it. One day, however, I noticed that the emptiness had become a delicate nectar reflecting the presence of a deep and all-pervasive peacefulness.

Two of my friends had a similar reaction to the one I'd experienced. Their concern eased somewhat when they learned they were not alone in their experience, that life feeling flat was not so unusual and perhaps even normal; there was really nothing wrong with them.

When the human body dies and the brain stops functioning, the EEG is said to "flatline." For the spiritual seeker there comes a time when the ego and free will are seen for what they are; illusions. It's as though the ego has taken poison; and although it might take a while, it has been administered a lethal dose. This profound understanding can give rise to the feeling that life has become flat and meaningless. This is the ego's flatline, and I'm happy to say, the associated depression is temporary.

Better news

To come to the conclusion, through personal observation, that there is no free will can be disturbing. It has, however, some unexpected benefits, not always apparent when dealing with the experience of flatline. To see this more clearly we'll look at a central aspect of meditation and its effect in the lives of those who practice. There are different forms of meditation but we'll use the one mentioned earlier, the one where breath is the gentle focus of attention, the mantra, so to speak. In the initial instructions the student is told to focus attention on the inhalation and exhalation of the breath and gently keep it there. The idea is to allow awareness to rest in the breath and not be distracted by anything. But, what typically happens?

Sitting quietly I hear the sound of a dog barking and it disturbs the process I'm engaged in. After a while I settle down again and return to an awareness of breathing where the attention is focused . . . for a few moments, at least! Then my nose itches; I try to ignore it but the itch becomes the focus of attention and I've forgotten all about the breath. Finally in exasperation I scratch my nose and return to the awareness of breathing. I stay with the breathing for a little while, only to realize I've become completely immersed in remembering a conversation I recently had with a neighbor. Noticing this, I return to the inhalation and exhalation of the breath. After a while my legs and back are aching and my attention is drawn away from breathing again. By and large I find the experience of meditation frustrating. My attention span is almost nonexistent. How will I ever reach the place where attention to breathing is primary?

The next time I meet with the meditation instructor I tell him of the trouble I'm having. "My mind is like a wild untrained monkey, doing exactly what it wants regardless of what I want." He chuckles and says, "You never realized this before? Now you do." "And, that's good?" I ask. "That's good," he responds. "What about the distractions?" I ask. "Simply allow everything to be as it is and gently bring the mind back to the breathing."

In the early stages of meditation the frustration level can be high until we take seriously the instructor's reminder that things happen; dogs bark, noses itch, legs fall asleep and thoughts carry us away. The key point to meditation is the ability to allow all these things to be as they are, to reach a point where we're no longer upset by the distractions, which are simply appearances on the screen of awareness. The focal point begins to shift, from originating in the personal awareness to originating in the impersonal awareness. When this happens in meditation it spills over into daily life. At first the effect of accepting whatever comes continues for a few minutes after meditation, and over time two or three minutes becomes fifteen minutes, half an hour, an hour and so on. When we persist with meditation there's a gradual expansion of the acceptance of *what is* in daily life. The hope is that eventually such acceptance becomes the norm. For this to happen, however, requires considerable dedication; sometimes ten or twenty years, and if you're anything like me, more. The gradual approach can be very gradual!

In the direct approach there's no engagement in spiritual discipline; the act of meditation, for instance, is rarely used. How then can the seeker come to accept life as it is? That state emerges directly from understanding itself, understanding that we do not have free will.

Since we don't have free will there's no sense in being upset with life because life simply happens as it does, regardless of what we want or do. The result is a deeper acceptance of life and our part in it.

What happens when I can't accept what is going on, despite understanding the lack of free will? Take for instance the following. A man I play soccer with makes a racist comment about someone we both know. I find myself getting angry with him and a heated argument ensues. Afterwards on my way home from the game I'm upset with myself. Why didn't I just leave things alone? Why didn't I just recognize his ignorance? After all, he couldn't help saying what he said because he doesn't have free will either.

My reaction is part of what is. Knowing I don't have free will means the reaction that took place within me couldn't be helped either; it simply happened. But, the fact is, I am upset by my reaction and find it hard to accept. That being so is a fact as well. Can I accept that? That is, can I accept the fact that I cannot accept my behavior at the moment?

What is happening here? What is happening is a deeper awareness of what it means to accept life as it comes. It does not simply mean accepting the events taking place in life and excluding myself as a participant in those events. I'm an integral part of life and my reactions are part of the mix, part of what is. So the question becomes, can I observe my own behavior in the same way I can observe another person's behavior? Can I accept my actions and reactions as readily as I can accept someone else's?

Generally speaking it is easier to accept things as they are when it doesn't involve us; that is, it's easier to accept the behavior of others and more difficult to accept our own. But as the understanding deepens concerning the lack of free will, our personal behavior becomes more and more obvious to us and more easily accepted for what it is . . . part of the inevitable expression of life. And, this awareness, this detachment, comes about purely as a result of understanding and without recourse to the lengthy process of meditation. The point is not that meditation isn't helpful, but rather that it is not essential. For those concerned about the lack of discipline there's some comfort in understanding this; this is good news, one of the benefits, believe it or not, of the deepening awareness of the lack of free will!

With the passage of time there's greater acceptance of the fact that the ego continues to function as it always has and there is nothing we can do about it. This is still disturbing but after a while, as acceptance settles in, it becomes more natural and spontaneous. In some ways the ego is like a recalcitrant child (someone else's child, of course!). Ramesh used to ask, "Who created the ego in the first place?" The answer, in a manner of speaking, is "God." Ramesh's response was always the same. "Since you have no free will and the ego was put there by God, then you might as well relax and know that God will remove it when and if the time comes." Even to understand this on an intellectual level is important, a beginning that matures over time into what might be called an understanding that rests in the heart.

••• The good news

Just because at this moment we realize free will is an illusion, doesn't mean the illusion has only just started. No. Free will has never existed from the time of our birth to the present moment. This means that all the choices we've made, all the decisions over which we've agonized, were simply part of a process that inevitably brought us to this place at this time. Sometimes we find ourselves at what are obvious crossroads in life. One particular instance stands out. I'd been offered a job which would have meant a move out of the community where I lived. What would I do? I hadn't a clue. I remember thinking that in six months time I would know what took place. Knowing I didn't have free will didn't always make things any easier.

Since there's no free will, how can there be any responsibility for our actions? I mean responsibility in the way the term is generally used: that I am liable one way or another for my decision; that is, if things turn out well I can be credited for my wisdom, and if they don't I can be blamed for my lack of wisdom. In other words, I would be the recipient of praise or blame. Of course, given the nature of the ego, I would do all within my power to deflect the blame elsewhere. But, without free will there's no room for praise or blame; it simply does not apply.

Let's come back to the word "responsibility." When we shed the burden of responsibility there's a shift from the heaviness of being responsible to the light ease of responding appropriately and effortlessly, within the framework or context of ongoing events. I would suggest this is perhaps a more accurate definition for the term "responsibility": namely, response ability, the ability to respond appropriately in whatever situation arises, given our makeup and characteristics and the context of ongoing events. It's as though we are simply a portion of an organic process that unfolds naturally; and thus the ego with its accompanying self-importance no longer stands out as the kingpin upon which such momentous decisions depend.

Does this mean we become irresponsible in our actions, that we fail to pay our debts or keep our word? No, it does not mean that. If anything, there's more attention to detail, and to keeping our word, keeping others informed, paying debts and being considerate of others. As the ego fades the natural characteristics and qualities of the person involved come easily to the surface. The need for praise and blame fades with the ego and we become responsive to others in more appropriate ways. That doesn't mean we'll always be sweetness and light. We may be firmer, more prepared to stand our ground than previously, as there's less concern about what others think of us.

The question arises, if we have no free will then why do anything? The answer is, of course, that we can't do nothing. We have to engage in some action, as we have since birth. The body requires physical action. We could put ourselves to bed, but in the end we'd still have to get up and go about our business, as the natural energy in the body would not allow us to be inactive.

When life is accepted as it is
There is no concern for the way things are
For when the world is loved as oneself
Everything is taken care of.

When the mouth is closed
Life is simply witnessed.

The sharp edges are smoothed away
The tangles unravel by themselves
The harsh glare fades
And the swirling dust
Settles by itself.

This is how the sage experiences
The harmony of life.

Lao Tzu

Chapter 10
Here and Now

The present moment

The fact that we have no free will, coupled with understanding the ego and how it functions—its tendency to generate melodrama and divide the seamlessness of life into good and bad—enables us to live increasingly in the present moment. This is a welcome break from the disturbance with which we are all too familiar when the mind propels us into painful recollections of the past and pointless and exaggerated worries about the future.

The more we experience the peace of the present moment the more we want to stay in it. The more we suffer from being in the mind the more we are repelled by it.

These two aspects, attraction and repulsion—because of the contrast between them—create, for a while, an increase in suffering that is difficult to bear. Because of this we settle more and more permanently into the present where peace can be found. The mind is then used for its correct purpose of efficiently taking care of the practical tasks before it, rather than wallowing in worry and drama about what has already happened and what might happen.

One day I had an argument with a friend. I didn't like what happened and was very upset with myself; my mind drove me crazy. I gathered a towel and swim fins and headed for the beach. Time to body surf. When I got to the beach I walked along not seeing it, completely lost in the mind. At the end of the beach I climbed out on some rocks, and only then, when it required my undivided attention, did I notice my surroundings. I felt as if I'd suddenly emerged from a dark oppressive place into the here and now. No longer lost in the mind, I saw the big beautiful waves, saw how the riptide would provide an easy return to deep water after riding the waves in.

Here and now

The melodramatic mind always takes us into the past and future where the self-referencing of the ego predominates. When aware of our surroundings we can be said to be in the present moment. The present moment is not the space between past and future, as it is often thought to be. Why? Because past and future exist only in memory, or projection based on memory. Past and future are not substantial; they lack the immediacy and aliveness that exist in the present moment. Furthermore, past and future are purely conceptual in nature and of necessity exist solely in the mind. The present moment is real and as such has a timeless quality to it. When the awareness is one with the present moment we are often surprised at the passage of time and refer to it with the idiom, "time flies." Suffering, however, takes place when the present moment is obscured by memories and thoughts, which relate to the mental states of past and future. These mental states are kingdoms over which the ego rules supreme. In the here and now there's no concern about what happened or might happen. In the present moment there may be things to do, or things happening, but what takes place simply takes place spontaneously within the field of consciousness.

It is this to which Lao Tzu refers when he says:

The master does not strive to accomplish great things
And so a great deal is accomplished.
When difficulty is encountered
He does not pretend it is not there.
He sees things as they are

Difficult or easy it makes no difference to him,
He knows that by facing facts
Difficulties are overcome.

When facts are not faced, when the present is not seen for what it is, a person enters the mind and in the mind there can be no peace. In the non-acceptance of the way things are, the ego presumes it can do better and complains that if it had been allowed to do what it wanted in the past, the present would be as desired. Because the present moment is not accepted, because it does not meet our expectations, we are disturbed—and that which is disturbed would have to be the ego. The ego lives in "what ifs" and "if only's." For the ego, the mind is real and the factual reality of events simply a mistake or something that any sensible person would reject. Since life changes all the time, the ego is in constant turmoil because it cannot accept what is, apart from the occasional times when what it wants and the events in the outer world coincide. At such times the ego claims credit for what has happened. When the ego's desires are met we are like the gambler who finally wins the jackpot. Because of those occasional wins the gambler in us, the ego, is hooked.

Werner Erhardt, the founder of the Erhardt Seminar Training (Est), asks: "What is the difference between a human being and a rat? If you place a piece of cheese in a maze the rat will find it. If you never place the cheese in the maze again the rat will eventually accept that the cheese is not to be found and stop looking for it. Human beings, on the other hand, have not learned this; they keep looking."

Real perfection appears flawed
Real fullness appears empty
Real straightness appears crooked
Real skill appears clumsy
Real eloquence appears awkward

And
The man of Tao
Masters the world
By allowing it to be . . .
As it is

Lao Tzu

CHAPTER 11

THE IDEA OF PERFECTION

THE INTRINSIC PERFECTION OF THE WHOLE

Human beings have looked forward to the day when life would be perfect and people of the world could live in peace. In the Christian tradition such a time is referred to metaphorically as the "New Jerusalem." When the pilgrims landed at Plymouth they hoped to establish peace and harmony in a new world; it would be, they hoped, the New Jerusalem. When we look at human history, however, life seems anything but perfect and peace a far off dream.

But, what about this idea of perfection, what about the idea that life could be perfect? As improbable as it seems, is there even a faint chance of such a possibility?

When we look at the idea of perfection it would seem to have as many interpretations as there are people and from this perspective alone, perfection upon which everyone could agree would be impossible to attain.

Could there perhaps be another way of approaching this idea? An approach not derived from an agreed upon definition of perfection but one grounded in another way of looking at life altogether.

A clue can be found in the Zen story of the woodcutter and his son. It goes something like this. An old woodcutter had a son and a beautiful stallion he used to help him haul wood. One night a number of wild mares passed by and the stallion broke out of the corral and joined them. The people of the village, hearing the news, went to see the woodcutter. "It's too bad your stallion has gone off with the wild mares," they said. The woodcutter looked at them and said, "We'll see."

That night the woodcutter heard a commotion out in the corral and went to see what was going on. The stallion had returned and brought with him three mares. In the morning the villagers came by to look at the new mares and said to the woodcutter, "How wonderful that the stallion has returned and you now have more horses." The old man looked at them and said, "We'll see."

A week later the son of the woodcutter, while trying to train one of the mares, was thrown off and broke his leg. The villagers, hearing what happened, came that evening to the woodcutter's home. "We're sorry your son has broken his leg. Now things will be much harder for you." The old man looked at them again and said, "We'll see."

The king was about to go to war with a neighboring country and sent his soldiers to every village in the kingdom looking for all the eligible young men to serve in the army. When they saw the woodcutter's son they passed him by because of his broken leg. That evening the villagers came again. "How fortunate that your son broke his leg when he did." The old man looked at the villagers and said, "We'll see.

Could it be that the perfection we have sought in life is not located in time or space but rather in a unique approach to life, something pointed to in the woodcutter story. That being the case consider this: Consider the possibility that life as it is, is already perfect. When looked at from this perspective we would come face to face with our firmly held opinions, those beliefs we hold to be true or seem so obvious as to be considered common sense. Such a view is clearly expressed by the villagers in the story above.

Perhaps the reader might try an experiment. For the next six months consider the possibility that life as it is, is already perfect. If that was the case what beliefs would he have to surrender in order to see the perfection present in every situation encountered?

For example, take someone who believes that life will always work out, that life is fair. What they really mean is that life will work out according to their wishes, their ideas as to what is the best outcome. This leads to a great deal of disappointment. But when the perfection of the whole is seen there is a shift and the person concludes that life is working out the way it is, regardless of beliefs and in this way unforeseen possibilities emerge.

Another example at the time of writing this might be considered. There is a massive oil leak in the Gulf of Mexico following the explosion and destruction of one of the BP oil rigs. This is a catastrophe for both human and wild life. Mr. Obama, seeing beyond the immediate situation, has suggested that the financial support given to the oil companies should be redirected to clean energy programs. By doing this he has used the catastrophe to create an opportunity for change, something that might not have been possible before.

If the reader can approach life in this manner for the next six months it would be interesting to ask what difference this has made in his life? Is there more turmoil, more disturbance or more peace? Is it possible to return to the old approach? I doubt it, unless of course there is a greater love of turmoil than peace.

You wish to improve the world?
I say it cannot be done!

The world is sacred.
Tamper with it and you'll ruin it
Possess it and you'll lose it.

Sometimes one is ahead
Sometimes behind
Sometimes life is difficult
Sometimes easy.

Lao Tzu

Chapter 12

Destiny & Dharma

Destiny and dharma

The story is told of Hitler standing with his generals on the coast of France in 1940 and looking across the Channel to England. On his mind was whether he should invade or not. His generals advised him to do so quickly while England was still weak and before it could regain its strength. Instead, Hitler turned away from England and sent his army into Russia where it was soundly defeated. He knew the opportunity before him and yet turned in another direction, one that led to his ultimate defeat. It is at times like this that we glimpse something momentous underway, something inevitable, something over which, even if we believed otherwise, we know we have no control whatsoever.

It is man's ego, his sense of self-importance, that makes him feel he has a hand in things. As the ego sinks into the background, however, he's left with the sense of being an intimate and integral part of what is happening, but certainly not the predominant instrument he took himself to be when his ego strutted across the stage.

A bulldozer works in a gravel pit and not on the ocean. By the same token, a sailboat works well on the ocean and not in a gravel pit. Design determines function. Michelangelo had certain characteristics or gifts that came with his birth. Those gifts played a significant role in what he was to become. Einstein had gifts peculiar to him that also played a determining role in the contributions he made to science and our understanding of the universe.

A rose is not a stinging nettle and certainly not a cottonwood. The design and function of a rose is to produce blossoms and to dispense its fragrance to all who happen by. The innate characteristics of objects, including the human object, largely determine what they become. This is known as the law of dharma, and when we no longer resist what happens there's an ease to life not present otherwise.

I used to work as a banquet waiter in a large hotel in Hawaii. We'd finished serving a five-course meal to twenty-five hundred people. It was one of those events where the guests were rushed in and out in less than an hour. We'd been busing plates for a couple of hours, carrying them to the kitchen to be washed and put away. One of my co-workers, a young Hawaiian, took a moment's break and, sitting down at one of the littered tables, let out a groan. I looked at him and saw what he was looking at. He was an intelligent man, gifted, and yet here he was surrounded by a sea of dishes that stretched endlessly into his future. If he didn't move in the direction of his natural abilities he'd be stuck doing what was below his capabilities.

Despite our gifts we may not fulfill those capacities because other constraints come into play—such things as the necessity of making a living or supporting a family, lack of education, geographical location, war, a lack of courage, and so on. Still, the overall tendency for all human beings is to feel the tug toward the fulfillment of their dharma, that for which they were designed.

What is the interplay between dharma and destiny? Dharma is that to which we are most naturally suited; whereas destiny is what actually took place, and this is known only at the end of one's life. While I was contemplating this question a rather unusual metaphor came to mind. It has to do with the power of nature to bring forth its designs—in this instance, the creation of life. The biological imperative ensures that the male body produces and releases millions of sperm with the sole intent of fertilizing the egg. It takes only one sperm to do this, and yet millions are produced and released.

Destiny in this instance is not that of an individual. It is not that one particular sperm is blessed; rather, the probability that pregnancy will result lies in the seeming overproduction of sperm, an impersonal function.

When we examine history we are able to detect certain patterns and collective movements that reflect the larger sweep of destiny. But, what of personal destiny, particularly in the light of dharma? Although dharma tends to move us in one direction rather than another, it is not an absolute determining factor in what takes place. Even though one's dharma may tend to create the probability, for instance, that we will enter a particular field of endeavor there's no guarantee it will happen. As was mentioned, most of us only become aware of our personal destiny at the end of our lives.

The Orchestra, the symphony, destiny and dharma

Life can be likened to a large orchestra playing a complex, beautiful and intricate symphony. People are assigned instruments, which are determined by the gifts that accompany their birth. Those suited to the drum are assigned to the percussion section; those suited to the violin are assigned to the string section, and so on. Although each participant in the orchestra is an individual and completely unique, each one is under the direction of the conductor. The conductor takes the unique characteristics of each instrument and each musician and creates a symphony. No two instruments are exactly alike and no two musicians respond to the music and the direction in the same way. When these elements are combined, however, the written music is given expression.

If one focuses on the individual musician it is easy to think of him as independent, and in a sense he is; it is easy to think he can operate separately, because he appears to do so. It is easy to mistake the actions of the musician for one who has free will. But when we step back from the focus on the individual and take a broader perspective, it becomes obvious that each musician is part of the whole orchestra. Each musician is involved in the translation of the written form of music into a collective melodic expression capable of being heard. Each independent musician, it turns out, is united by a common desire to give expression to the music he sees before him.

What the musician plays is music written before the performance. What he reads and what he plays is something already determined; he is in a sense simply following directions.

In daily life we discover the music written in the heart of each and every one of us. The composer and conductor of the symphony are what we refer to as God, the Tao, or simply, Consciousness Itself. What emerges is the exquisite symphony we refer to as life, with all of its power, beauty, discordance, pathos, suffering and bliss.

• • • Silence is the source of all sound

Astronomers have taken the movement of the planets and through sophisticated instruments turned those movements into sound. What results is what might be called the music of the spheres. If we took all the events taking place on the planet and assigned particular frequencies to them we'd find another kind of music taking place. If we were able to do this with literally everything in the universe we'd have absolute silence. Lao Tzu states, "Silence is the source of all sound." What does he mean? To understand this let us work backwards.

Some of the newer more expensive cars being built today are silent inside. Outside sounds, road noise, engine noise and transmission noise are all absent. How is this accomplished? Sensitive computers detect a particular sound frequency, which of course is a wave pattern. The computer generates a wave pattern of its own exactly opposite that of the sound it has detected. The two waves cancel each other out and sound is thus eliminated.

The orchestra of life with which each of us is involved is experienced from a particular perspective, our own. If we were able to hear all the sounds ever created in the universe from the perspective of the whole, the sounds would cancel each other out and the eternal silence would remain. Once more Lao Tzu sums it up in this way:

And, when it's all over
It's as if nothing ever happened.
In an instant,
Like the clap of hands,
The rivers of time
Have vanished in the ocean of the Tao.

Conversely, when it all begins the universe emerges from the silence and the great Om; the great symphony is born.

Before time ever was,
The great Tao existed
Silent and unmoving.

Then suddenly It moved
For no reason
The potential became actual
And the vast universe was born.

Lao Tzu

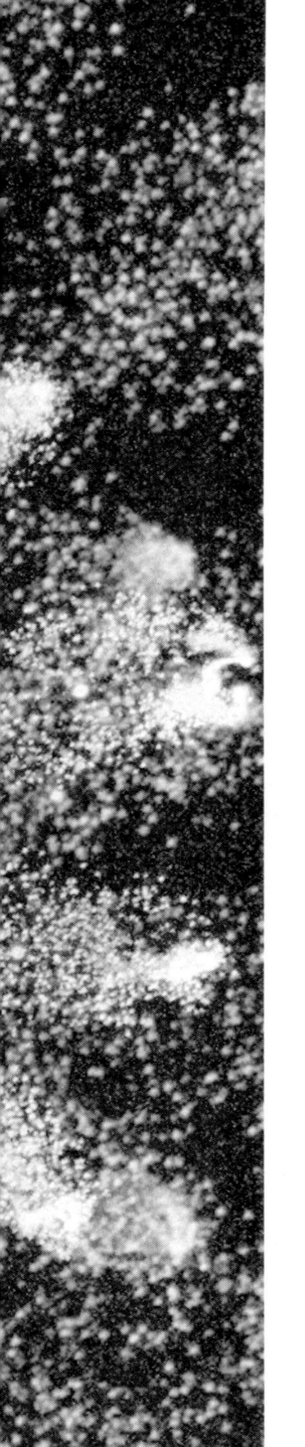

Chapter 13
Models For Cause & Effect

The Newtonian Perspective

In the preceding discussion of destiny and dharma the issue of cause and effect comes to the fore. Newtonian physics suggested the universe could be likened to a clock wound up by the Creator. What resulted was thought to be predictable, logical and linear, a simple but relatively obvious cause-and-effect relationship between individual events and people. This kind of perspective is still prevalent in Western society today. We are constantly asking ourselves what caused an event to take place; really we are asking what cause preceded the current effect. For instance, "How did you come to read this book at this time?" Can you identify all those things, the thoughts and events that led you to being where you are at this moment? Can you identify the cause, as we tend to speak and think of it? When we examine what brought us to this place at this time there are any number of factors.

The Buddhist perspective

The Buddhists' approach to this question is quite different. The idea of cause and effect is accepted, but it is not the linear cause and effect proposed by Newton. To my mind it is more realistic, more rooted in what happens in life.

Imagine a large hall in which thousands of tiny mirrors are hung in every possible direction and at every possible height. In the hall there are also thousands of diamonds hanging from the ceiling all at different levels. Imagine a burst of light entering the hall from a single point. What would happen? The light would be reflected, and refracted in the case of the diamonds, bouncing off other mirrors and refracted by other diamonds. It would be virtually impossible to tell where things began or what caused what in any linear manner.

Lao Tzu, the Chinese sage said, "*What happens,happens, and no one knows why, not even the sage.*" Though there are certain trends that seem to be true and predictable, those trends cannot be used to predict with absolute certainty individual events for individual people.

••• The Quantum possibility perspective

Quantum physics suggests that consciousness itself is the primary cause of events taking place. The unknown potential, the realm of quantum possibilities, is determined at the moment that consciousness is brought to bear. Prior to this moment it is simply a potential for many different combinations of possibilities. The experiments arising from Quantum Physics produce virtually the same understanding as the insights of Advaita Vedanta, and Taoism.

This perspective has a profound impact on modern science and philosophy but is largely absent from the Newtonian model still used by most of us in our day-to-day lives. Perhaps it is just a matter of time before it percolates down. Despite our lack of familiarity with much of it we are already under its effect.

In trying to understand the inability to always accurately predict specific events, Heisenberg developed the theory of indeterminacy, upon which the law of probability is based. Statistical charts suggest a certain percentage of the population in a given city will be murdered, a certain percentage of boys will be born in January and another percentage of girls will be born in February. Insurance tables are based on the same notion of statistical probability. Dogs will bite a fixed percentage of mail delivery men in any given year; a fixed percentage of men working in a coal mine will die of black lung disease; and so on. Why do these numbers vary so little over time? Why are insurance tables capable of prediction based on statistical probability? Why can they predict, for instance, that 40% of men at the age of sixty will have a particular kind of cancer, but not who those men will be?

We are in some ways obtaining a more accurate description of how the physical universe works; yet as we do, it becomes more ephemeral, more of a mystery, less and less certain. Big surprise!

To understand that our problem is the mind, not theoretically but totally, is true intelligence.
Ramesh Balsekar

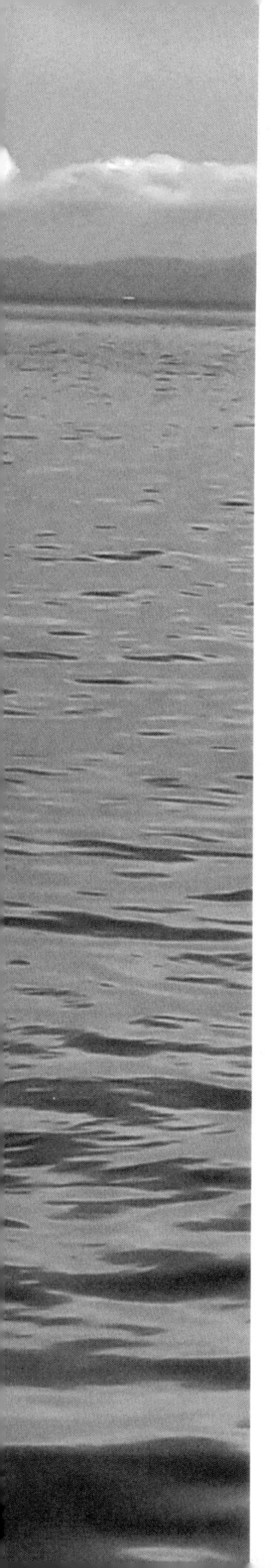

CHAPTER 14

THE NATURE OF THE MIND

THE MIND OF THE MONKEY

We speak of the mind with such certainty, but what actually is the mind? Is it an object located in time and space, like one's brain? Once more we are dealing with concepts; and just as the ego is nothing more than a concept, so also is the mind. In fact it could be stated that the mind and the ego are, for all intents and purposes, one and the same.

But, for the sake of this inquiry let's say that the defining characteristic of the mind is that it must think. We can get an inkling of this from the Zen idea of "no mind," which points to the absence of thought; its opposite. When thought begins, the mind comes into being. There are times in life when we experience no thought, and at those times there really is "no mind," and no me. But when the mind is present, thinking must take place.

If I'm to paint a house I must calculate the square footage, then determine the amount of paint per square foot, the preparation needed, the colors to be used, the kind of paint, the length of ladders, and the selection of other tools and equipment. All of this must be planned in order to meet a particular deadline. To do this requires the use of the mind. To use the mind in this way is to use what the sage Ramesh Balsekar refers to as the "working mind." It is the working mind that comes into play when we book a plane ticket, repair an engine, or produce a piece of pottery. When the working mind is functioning there is no me or identified consciousness present. When the mind is not engaged in this useful activity it falls back into what Ramesh calls the "thinking mind," or what I prefer to call the "melodramatic mind."

The melodramatic mind is engaged in the process of self-referencing. That is, all events and conversations are looked at from the perspective of me. In this frame of mind I continually ask myself, what effect will these things have on me, what does this or that mean about me, who is doing this to my friend, and so on. Such a mind is completely preoccupied with the self, the personal consciousness. It is the personal consciousness that divides the world into good and bad, people we like and people we don't . . . certainly the basis for gossip and soap opera, is it not?

The story is told of a king who was given a gift of two monkeys, which were kept in small cages. The king immediately ordered his chief minister to enclose an area of land that contained trees. He was instructed to create a rich environment for the monkeys with swings and places to climb. The chief minister assembled his men and they set to work. In two weeks they'd finished the project and the king released the monkeys into the compound. The minister had noticed that not once did the king allow the monkeys out of the cages during the construction. Curious, he inquired why. The king responded. "You don't understand the nature of monkeys, do you? They need something to do, something that will keep them occupied in a creative, challenging and interesting way. Without that they become destructive of both their environment, themselves and each other." In the East the symbol for the mind is the monkey.

What then, can be done to rid ourselves of the melodramatic mind? Nothing! There's nothing we can do, for two reasons. Who we take ourselves to be, the one who would rid us of the melodrama, is nothing but a concept and therefore not real: we do not exist. And if we did exist we still wouldn't have free will.

In Buddhist thought there's the concept of the witness, that which observes all events, thoughts, and reactions. What, then, is this witness? Is it not the underlying impersonal consciousness that has accompanied us from birth? When the impersonal consciousness is primary and the ego absent, understanding takes place. That understanding can be the event known as enlightenment or a flash of insight that contributes to the awakening process. As the understanding deepens, changes in behavior take place that bring greater peace and harmony.

Take, for example, attachment. When we understand that attachment is the source of all suffering, it generally means there'll be less tendency to be attached, and should attachment occur, less chance it will endure.

Understanding brings spontaneous and appropriate changes in behavior. This is true when it comes to understanding attachment and it's also true when it comes to understanding the mind and its two predominant forms of expression, the functional working aspect and the dysfunctional melodramatic aspect. Understanding the nature of the mind is helpful in becoming free of the dysfunctional aspect.

A friend of mine was working on a large project. The man for whom he was doing the work loved the exercise of authority, his authority. His conversations with my friend were largely one-way: he held forth on his soapbox, while my friend listened. His attitude was condescending, as though speaking to a child, and when it came to women this condescension was palpable. As he saw it, women had their place and it was to serve his interests, and failing that they should be silent or leave.

My friend was told his wife could no longer be on the site because she'd had the audacity to stand up for herself and support him. This proved disturbing and throughout the day he seemed preoccupied. When we spoke it was obvious and understandable that the self-referencing aspect of his mind was pummeling him. He was completely absorbed in conversations in his mind over the events that had taken place—what he could have done differently, what he might do next, and so on. So deeply immersed was he that there was no escape and he suffered as a result. Why did he suffer? He wanted things to be other than the way they were. He wanted the man not to be such an ass and he wanted to be free of his mind, and to both desires he was attached.

Here's another example that can make this dilemma clear. I get on a bus and take my seat. I open a novel and before long I'm lost in the world of the author's and my imagination. After half an hour I look up, only to realize I've passed my stop. I get off at the first chance and wait for a bus going the other way. When it comes I get on, this time paying attention to what is going on, and not getting immersed in the novel. Being immersed in the novel is like being immersed in the mind.

There is a beautiful Buddhist story that gives a clear illustration of how the mind works and of its love of melodrama. Two Buddhist monks were walking along a mountain trail one morning when they came to a stream swollen and dangerous from snowmelt. They noticed a young woman standing at the stream's edge with a look of consternation on her face. The older monk immediately understood the situation. She was understandably afraid of the water, given her small size. He politely offered to carry the woman across and she accepted. Once on the other side the monk put her down and, making sure she had her belongings, bade the woman good day before continuing. Hours passed and the younger monk maintained a stony silence, something out of character for him. Suddenly in the late afternoon he broke his silence and in an angry voice accused the older monk of breaking his vow of chastity. The old monk burst out laughing, which only increased the vehemence of the accusations. He raised his hand in a gesture of silence and when the young monk became quiet said to him, "When I carried the woman across the stream I put her down on the other side and left her there. You, on the other hand, have been carrying her all day."

I used to work as a psychologist, and sometimes some unusual things happened with clients. One client, a twenty-two-year-old man, came to see me. He was borderline schizophrenic. When he entered my office he started talking, and not once did he make eye contact. His talking was incessant and made repetitive loops. There was no place for me to interrupt him. After several minutes I sank down in my chair until I slid onto the floor, watching his eyes the whole time. He suddenly stopped talking and looked closely at me, making eye contact for the first time. Then we began to converse. Later I found it helpful to meet him near his home. We would hike into the mountains. I took him into places where there was a level of danger and one had to pay attention. As we traversed those areas he became silent. His attention was riveted to his surroundings and thus free of the mind. Once we reached our destination we would sit quietly in a glade and listen to the sound of the birds or the wind through the trees. At times like this I could offer him a little help.

I drift like a wave on the ocean
Aimless as the restless wind.
I have no desire but the absence of desire
I am sustained and nourished
By the breasts of the Great Mother.
Lao Tzu

Chapter 15
Understanding The Whole Process

Raindrops—A metaphor to understand the whole process

Wind sweeps across the ocean, and the sun combines with the wind to evaporate some of the water, which rises and then condenses, forming clouds. As the temperature cools at higher elevations, the particles of moisture join with each other to form distinct drops of rain which, being heavy, begin to fall. Each raindrop as it falls encounters changes of temperature, fluctuations in wind, dust particles, buffeting and so on. When the raindrops reach the end of their journey they enter the ocean and vanish. What is it that has vanished? The water that comprised each raindrop has not vanished; all that has vanished is the form, the shape and texture. The raindrop as distinct and separate from the ocean, from other raindrops and other objects, has vanished; that is all.

Human life is similar to the life of a raindrop. The impersonal consciousness is of the same substance, so to speak, as the Totality of Consciousness, and it is this impersonal consciousness which is the heart of human existence. The human being is an object in the phenomenal world, the world of form; he is separate, and like the raindrop, during his lifetime he encounters many changes. Upon death the human being returns to the Totality of Consciousness, much as the raindrop enters and is absorbed by the ocean.

In the human being we have the development of the ego, which becomes the focal point of experience. The ego in a sense expropriates for itself the underlying impersonal consciousness without which life would not exist. This would be similar to the raindrop developing an ego, which would in the end mean nothing. Despite its pretensions, the raindrop eventually becomes one with the ocean. Even rain that falls on land eventually reaches the sea.

In the human being, however, the ego has a very strong desire to continue its existence. As a result it has created religious belief systems concerning life, and life after death. From the Christian perspective life continues in the form of a soul in either heaven or hell. From the perspective of some Eastern traditions we have the belief in reincarnation. Although most Buddhists believe in reincarnation, it was not something Buddha taught. In fact, he explicitly stated there is no individual to reincarnate.

The ego enjoys life and does not want it to end at death. Instead it comes to believe in life after death. But, who is it that hopes to survive death? Another ego believes in reincarnation. But again, who is it that desires to reincarnate?

Now, this is where it gets tricky concerning reincarnation. Who is it that reincarnates? Is it Bill, Joan, Pat, Nassir, Robert, Michelle or David? From the perspective of David, he's only interested in David's life, not who he might have been in earlier incarnations when he was a different person. Surely this must be the ego that seeks to live on. Let's return for a moment to the raindrop. What can be said to have happened to all of the experiences of all the raindrops over time? The raindrops and their experiences would be dispersed throughout the ocean and thus could be said to still exist. When the water evaporates and begins the cycle of life and death again, all those memories of life experiences must be present in the water vapor that eventually becomes more raindrops. A more accurate understanding of this can be found in the idea of the hologram. No matter how many times a holographic negative is cut, each piece retains all the information, quite unlike a regular negative which loses whatever information is cut away. The ocean and the hologram used as metaphors here are what is meant by the Akashic Records, or what from the Christian perspective is known as the "Book of Life" or the "Book of Remembrances."

There's considerable writing and information concerning those who remember past lives. If there is no reincarnation, what is going on? Could it be that the lives these people remember are recalled simply because they have access, as do we all, to the holographic information stored in the ocean of Consciousness, the Akashic Records? This information is written deep within all of us, but it is not the record of any individual who has reincarnated, it is just the memories of all the raindrops. It is incarnation not reincarnation! Individuality is not transferred from one life to another. There is no individual to reincarnate. This is bad news for the ego.

The Universe—A story

Adapted from the Sufi tradition comes the following story.

By the time Nanoose the gnat graduated from college he'd earned the nickname, "Nanoose the Intelligent." Being smart, he soon had a job and did very well, earning a new nickname, "Courteous Intelligent Nanoose."

One day, Nanoose met the girl of his dreams. He started looking for a more upscale place to take his new bride. After all, he now had more than just himself to care for. After considerable searching he eventually settled upon the ear of a great elephant.

The new home was spacious and warm, with a great view, and when Nanoose showed it to his bride she agreed. Before long they settled in their new quarters and a large family was born and raised. Nanoose experienced the normal highs and lows of life, but his intelligence and courteousness helped ease the rough spots.

Nanoose was a secularist, wanting nothing to do with the foibles and pettiness of organized religion. He observed the laws of common decency and consideration for others. He was in no need of religious coercion or encouragement; he was quite beyond that.

As the years passed Nanoose rose to the top of his company, becoming the CEO. When the kids had grown and left, the home was bigger than they needed. It was, however, hard to leave a place filled with such warm memories of family and friends.

After due consideration Nanoose concluded that the positive reasons for finding a new home outweighed the negative ones; so for good and sufficient reasons it was decided to move.

Nanoose and his wife found a small place some distance away; a sow's ear, warm and more suitable. On the last day at his old home, when everything was packed and loaded, Nanoose stood in the passageway of the elephant's ear and recalled the first day he'd stood there, so many years ago. He'd drawn himself up to his full height, inhaled deeply and then as loudly as he could he'd projected his voice down the elephant's ear.

"Know this, Mr. Elephant. It is I, Nanoose the Intelligent, speaking. I have chosen your ear to live in. My wife and I will move in tomorrow and hope to raise a family. Out of courtesy for your kind generosity, I thought I should let you know of my intentions and ask if you have any objections." Nanoose listened carefully but no audible response was heard.

Now, years later, Nanoose stood at the same spot and contemplated his words of farewell. Once more he drew himself up to his full height and taking a deep breath shouted: "Oh mighty Elephant, it is I, Nanoose the Courteous, Nanoose the Intelligent, speaking to you for the last time. Thank you for providing a safe and warm home, a place where I raised a family with my wife. We've decided to leave, but thought it only courteous to inform you of our reasons. We are saddened to leave; but, as you know, time moves on, changes take place and one must do what one must do. We found something more suitable to our reduced needs. According to the honorable tradition of all intelligent gnats, I wish to thank you and wish you well. I know it's short notice but we've always found you most accommodating." With the last ounce of his strength Nanoose drew in another deep breath and yelled as loudly as he could. "Be well, great Elephant and thank you. May your life without us be as fulfilling as it was with us."

Nanoose cupped his hands to his ears and listened intently. The only sounds he could hear were his own labored breathing and the blood pulsing through his ears. For a moment he wondered if the elephant had heard him. Then shaking his head to get the buzzing out of his ear, the elephant let out a loud trumpeting, deep and resonant. Picking himself up, Nanoose turned on his heel and left the place that had been his home for so long. He was confident the elephant had heard him and the loud trumpeting he interpreted as a fond farewell and a sincere wish that he and his wife would be well in their new home. He found great comfort in this thought.

A metaphor for time

Time is an idea we have difficulty with. Imagine a large house filled with furniture and a myriad of objects. It is night and dark. All the objects already exist in the house but we cannot see them. Fortunately we have a flashlight, consciousness. We enter the house with the aid of the light. As we shine the light it illuminates the different objects and they're registered in consciousness. As we move through the house the light illuminates more objects, which then fade from awareness as we move on. Although all the objects are already present, they are perceived in sequence, one after the other, and this creates the illusion of time.

• • • The primary duality

The Tao gives birth to One
One gives birth to two
Two gives birth to three
And three to the ten thousand things.
Lao Tzu

Just as there's duality in the phenomenal world which enables us to perceive the objects around us, there's a kind of prior duality as well. It is the duality existing between the noumenal and the phenomenal, between the potential and the actual. The noumenal can be referred to as the grand potential, an undifferentiated possibility. In quantum physics the undifferentiated possibility becomes actual; it appears as a phenomenal object at the moment consciousness is brought to bear. This is the primary duality from which all other dualities derive.

The heavens and the earth are unreal
The ten thousand things an illusion.
To the sage, life's but a dream
And all mankind
Characters dreamed by the Tao.
Lao Tzu

Chapter 16
Maya

What is real?

The idea of illusion brings forth its opposite, the idea of what is real. There's a definition of "real" sometimes used in philosophy and often in Advaita. According to this definition, what is real is that which persists; that which does not persist is not real. What is it that always fits this definition of real? There are several terms used for it: God, the noumenal, potential energy, quantum possibility, even the void. Since every object in the phenomenal world is subject to decay, death and dissolution, it cannot be said to persist, and therefore, according to this definition, cannot be real. The phenomenal world, the world in which we live, is therefore not real; it is known as "Maya."

There's a Zen statement that says: At first rivers and mountains are real, then rivers and mountains are not real, and finally rivers and mountains are both real and unreal. What is the Zen master speaking about? What he's referring to is three stages associated with spiritual awakening. When the spiritual seeker begins his journey he, like most of us, takes the world to be real. The desk is real, the floor is real, the trees and water are real, the bus and the train are real, and so on. In one form or another this is the definition generally accepted within our culture. What do we mean by this?

What we mean is that the objects mentioned have substance, density, and solidity. They can be touched and clearly perceived for what they are, or so we believe.

When we look at a sliver of wood under a powerful microscope we see electrons rotating around a centrally located nucleus. These separate objects, the electrons and the nucleus, occupy a small portion of a large space of emptiness. In many ways this resembles the solar system. What we've taken to be real and solid is, as it turns out, not as solid, or as real, as we thought.

Some mystics have understood this without the aid of a microscope, as their vision and understanding were clear. Shamans and the Kahunas of Hawaii developed the capacity to slip from one world into another; and throughout history there have been those who arrived at the same conclusions. In some traditions certain mushrooms and herbs were used to penetrate the apparent solidity of life and see it for what it was: energy, patterns of energy. Rivers and mountains are no longer real.

A story is told of a sage instructing a king, a deep spiritual seeker, on this precise point. The sage had explained to the king the illusory nature of the world, when suddenly a wild elephant broke into the compound and threatened those inside. Everyone, including the sage, ran for safety. After the elephant left, the king asked the sage why he'd run away, particularly since the sage understood the elephant was not real. The sage responded that although the elephant was illusory, that is, not real, it was as real as it gets.

As the spiritual seeker reaches the second stage of the process, his belief in the reality of things is undermined. In life there are different events that have the capacity to dislodge him from the agreement he shares with those around him concerning reality. It might come as a result of illness, mystical experience, the use of certain herbs such as peyote or ayahuasca, or certain meditative practices. For others, the shared agreement learned early in life as part of the endarkenment or acculturation process is not as deeply rooted as in most people.

When the apparent solidity of the phenomenal world is seen for what it is, it can be unsettling. The very underpinnings of our lives, the assumptions we've taken for granted are thrown into question—uprooted, as it were, by understanding itself. The effects of this can sometimes be mistaken for mental illness. A large number of psychiatrists and psychologists inhabit a world they believe is real; solid, that is. They are "firm believers" (pun intended!). Either way, the seeker comes to understand that what he's taken to be real is not what it seems. As time goes on the questioning goes deeper and he comes to see different aspects of the illusory nature of life. Things that he's taken for granted have dissolved. The questions drive the understanding deeper until at last he understands that although life is an illusion, a grand one, it is still as real as it gets. Rivers and mountains are both real and unreal. That is, he must now act in life as he's always done, as though it is real; if he stands in front of a moving bus he must get out of the way or suffer the consequences, which are quite real . . . and at the same time, not real.

• • • Do you have my water yet?

This story from India might help in understanding the nature of Maya and its hypnotic power. Maya means illusion and refers to the world in which we live. The story goes something like this.

One day, God goes for a walk. He's indistinguishable from any of the people hurrying by. A man, sitting at the side of the road watching, sees God and, recognizing him for who he is, asks if he can walk with him. God agrees. After half an hour they leave the town and enter a deep forest. God looks at the man and says, "You may ask one question and I'll answer it for you." The man thanks him and they continue on their way. After a while the man says, "I have it! Show me Maya." "All right," says God, "I'll show you Maya."

By late afternoon they enter a clearing and God sits down to rest. "I'm thirsty," he says. "Would you get me some water please?" The man sets off along the path. It leads out of the forest and he finds himself looking across a valley of undulating fields. A broad muddy river winds its way slowly through the bottomland. On the far side of the river, beside a bridge, sits an old farmhouse. The valley runs parallel to a broad expanse of foothills that extend toward a ridge of high mountains. As he looks closely he can see that the river emerges into the valley from a deep cut in the foothills, a narrower valley originating in the mountains.

Crossing the bridge, he walks to the farmhouse and knocks on the door. A stunningly beautiful woman opens the door and he's immediately smitten. He courts her and eventually she consents to be his wife. Her parents, who are getting on in years, are the owners of the farm. Before long the farm is turned over to the young couple. Several years pass and they have two children. The extended family get along well and all contribute to the running of the farm.

One late spring the man climbs the sloping field toward the forest, one of his favorite vantage points. Winter has been severe and the snow pack on the mountain is deeper than he's seen before. The last several days have been exceptionally hot with unsettled weather, severe thunderstorms and dark, billowing clouds in an otherwise pristine sky. Looking toward the mountains he sees a violent storm raging along their flank. Lightning flashes and thunder shakes the air. He watches, fascinated. After a while he notices an unusual roar coming from the cut in the foothills. He searches for its source and is shocked by what he sees. A wall of water is surging down the ravine; the river meandering through the valley has started to swell and move more swiftly. Racing toward the farm, he crosses the bridge, yelling for his family. They rush for higher ground, but too late, a wall of water sweeps them away. The grandparents are the first to disappear. The husband and wife hold on to each other and the children, but one by one the young ones are torn from their grasp. Desperately the couple cling to each other, but the turbulence and force of the water is too great, and the man watches helplessly as his wife is sucked beneath the surface and vanishes.

An hour later he finds himself lying on a sandy shore under a hot sun. He is devastated with his loss and has no desire to live. Why was he spared? Suddenly he hears a familiar voice asking, "Do you have my water yet?"

The actor

Imagine you're an actor. You've been cast in a complex play involving numerous characters. You learn your lines and become thoroughly familiar with the role, which is full of pathos, melodrama, conflict and resolution; it is a hero's story. The name of the character you play is David O'Hearn, and your real name is Michael MacManus. The play is hugely successful and becomes well known. You spend several years playing Broadway to sold-out crowds. The play is so popular the cast goes on a world tour that lasts ten years. Imagine that at the end of this long run you've forgotten your real name; you've forgotten you were called Michael MacManus. Instead you now think of yourself as David O'Hearn, with all his attendant characteristics and his approach to life. The role you've played for so long is now yours. You've become the character and forgotten you're only an actor.

Could it be this is how life is? Could it be we've forgotten we're playing a role; we've forgotten who we are? Now, that is magic!

The mind does not distinguish

When we look at the mountains, the visual stimulus creates an impression in the mind. The fact that I mentioned the mountains and you did not visually see them doesn't matter because the stimulus of the word conjures in the mind an image of mountains drawn from past experience. For all intents and purposes the mind does not distinguish between the visual and the verbal stimulus. In both instances it sees mountains. But this confusion can be problematic, as can be seen from the following scenario.

I'm visiting a distant city, one I've never been to before. One morning I go for a walk and find myself in a wealthy section of town. Here, instead of houses there are mansions. I notice an old Rolls Royce coming toward me. It turns into a driveway and stops in front of the door. White Corinthian columns support a roof that extends over the driveway and entrance to the mansion. As the car comes to a stop a uniformed driver gets out and opens the door, and a man with a black mustache and shoulder-length hair gets out. He's wearing blue jeans, sandals, a Harris tweed jacket, a black wide-brimmed hat, and carrying a brown leather briefcase. As he approaches the front door, it opens and a butler greets him with a slight bow. The butler takes the man's hat and ushers him into the house, closing the door behind him. The chauffeur pulls ahead to a parking area, turns off the engine and gets out. Leaning against the front fender, he lights a cigarette and looks around.

What was just described is all that happened, the facts. When this story is told and listeners are asked to explain the events described, their responses tend to reflect one of a number of themes. The man in the Rolls Royce was the owner of the mansion and is a wealthy rock star being driven home; or the man was a drug dealer bringing a briefcase of money to pay for drugs; or he was a member of the mafia making a payment to the crime boss.

The mind draws conclusions from what it observes; and those conclusions, when added to the factual events taking place, are taken to be real, to be fact.

This characteristic of the mind contributes to the personal melodrama, which the ego loves. What we called beginner's mind originates in its source, the impersonal consciousness, and as such its perception is clear and uncontaminated. When the ego comes into play, however, perception has an explanation attached to it, and what had formerly been accurate now becomes questionable at best. One's perceived "reality" now reflects the self-referencing nature of the ego, it's commentary or explanation. The ego doesn't like the unknown; it thinks it has all the answers, or at least the best, most intelligent hypotheses. Unless a person is alert to what is happening he will not distinguish between the event and the thoughts about the event. A humorous story illustrates this point.

A man is driving home when he has a flat tire. It is late; he is deep in the country and no one is about. He doesn't have a flashlight and must feel around in the trunk for the jack. After a thorough search he remembers he doesn't have it. He was using the jack at home to replace a post under his deck and forgot to put it back in the trunk. What is he going to do? It's three o'clock in the morning and no one will be awake. He looks around and, in the distance a mile or so down the road, sees a light. “Nobody will help me at this hour,” he thinks. “If I knock on the door and wake people up, they’re liable to call the police and I’ll end up spending the rest of the night in a cell.” But, with no alternative he starts walking in the direction of the light. As he gets closer he sees that it comes from a farm. “Damn,” he thinks, “a farm usually has dogs. I’ll never get near, and if I do I’m liable to be bitten.” Arriving at the entrance to the farm, he turns up the driveway, and through the trees another light appears. As he gets closer he can see it comes from a front window of the house. Seated at the table, reading, is a woman dressed in a housecoat. “What a bummer,” he thinks, “a woman will never answer the door at this time of night, and if she does she’ll never lend me a jack.” He climbs the stairs and knocks on the door. The woman answers the door, and looking at the man asks him kindly how she can help. The man yells at her, “Keep your damned jack!” and turning on his heel, stamps down the steps and angrily stalks down the driveway.

And, when it's all over
It's as if nothing ever happened.
In an instant
Like the clap of hands
The rivers of time
Have vanished in the ocean of the Tao.
Lao Tzu

Chapter 17
Nothing Really Happened

Life, capricious & unfair

For many years I struggled with the issue of suffering. It seemed to me there was a lot of it in both my immediate and extended family. A great deal came from two World Wars and some from the lives of my family after the war. Life appeared capricious, unfair and unpredictable. There seemed little apparent cause-and-effect relationship between events. By the time I went to university in Boston I could no longer reconcile my experiences with a belief in God, and became an agnostic.

The problem of suffering continued to bother me. It was an irritant in the background of my life, always present, always unresolved. I talked with Ramesh about it. He asked if I dreamed. Obviously I did. He said that in our dreams there are rivers and mountains thousands of years old, old men dying, babies being born, people making love and people making war. In short, everything that happens in our daily life also happens in our dreams, including suffering. "What can be said to happen to the suffering experienced by those in our dreams?" he asked. The answer is, of course, nothing. Since the characters were not real, the suffering was also not real!

At once everything resolved itself, and the issue of suffering vanished. I saw that life was a grand cosmic dream, dreamed by the Source. The manifestation of life, the phenomenal world around us was as unreal and as real as our dreams. In much the same way that we dreamed our dreams at night, the Source or God dreamed the universe into existence through each and every sentient being. Ramana Maharshi, the Advaita sage of Arunachala, said that the highest teaching, the highest understanding was, "Nothing really happened."

Nothing really happens in our dreams. They are wonderful or terrifying occurrences but in the end nothing has happened. We go to a movie and watch the suffering, injury and death of the characters and are deeply moved, but what can really be said to have happened? Nothing. Human beings are great creators; in fact, the Old Testament says that man is made in the image and likeness of God. What this means is that human beings share the same characteristic, so to speak, the same inherent ability to create. We create rockets, radios, phones, cars and movies. In movies we project a visual story that appears very real to us. We are impressed with the realism but we still must use technology in the form of cameras and projectors. Dreaming, on the other hand, only requires the presence of the dreamer, consciousness itself.

The master makes no effort
To be wise
It never crosses his mind.
Free of illusion
And with no will of his own
He dwells in reality.
Lao Tzu

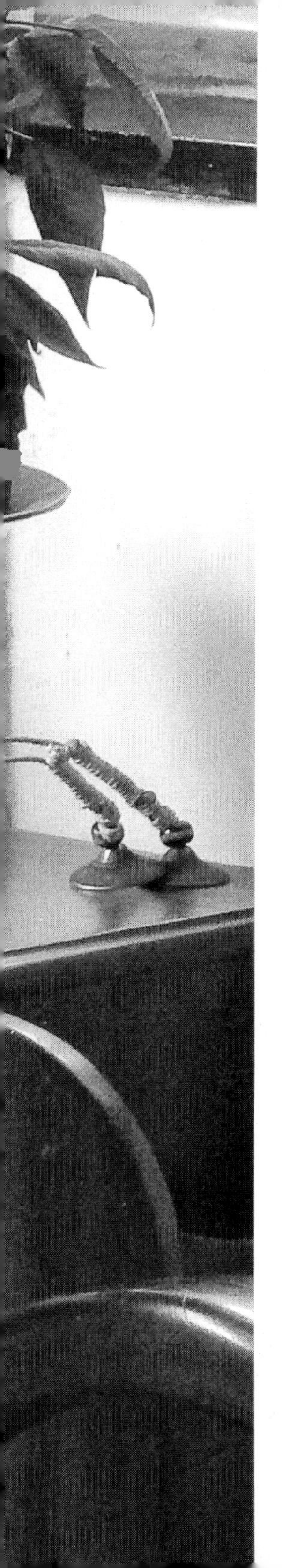

Chapter 18

The Guru

The difference between a teacher & a guru

In the West there is a tendency to look upon the word guru with some measure of embarrassment, preferring instead to use the term teacher. In the East, however, the teacher and the guru fulfill two completely different roles. The teacher helps the student obtain methods, theories and proficiency. In other words the teacher helps the student acquire information. The word guru, on the other hand, means dispeller of darkness, or dispeller of illusion. Because this is his role, the guru does not help the disciple acquire anything; instead he helps to undermine the conditioning and assumptions, which govern everything the disciple does and about which he is largely unaware. In doing so the guru undermines the cultural hypnosis and enables the disciple to break free of it. Nothing is acquired and the byproduct is peace of mind.

Lao Tzu refers to this when he says:

To understand life it is not necessary
To know a great deal.
No need to look at the world through a microscope
Or the heavens through a telescope.

Much learning gets in the way
And the more one knows the less one understands.

••• What is the guru?

Lost in the desert, consumed by thirst, I climb a steep rise and peer over the ridge of a sand dune. There before me, palm trees cluster around water that sparkles in the rose-colored rays of the setting sun. I run to the water and slake my thirst. What saves my life is the water. As long as I live, I will never forget the beauty of the oasis in which I found the water that saved my life.

The guru is the oasis. It was in his presence that the life-giving water was made available. The water that saved my life was the underlying truth, what in the Hindu tradition is known as the Sat Guru. It is the living truth within each one of us; that which is obscured by the ego's obsession. The Sat Guru, the Holy Spirit, our Buddha nature, the Tao, all of it is the same. All of it is love; all of it is written in our hearts, all of it is never really lost. Lao Tzu sums it up beautifully when he says,

The Tao of which we speak
Is hidden to the eyes of ordinary men,
It is hidden where it can never be found,
It is the essence of life,
The Ultimate Subject,
Consciousness Itself!

How do I know this?

It is what I am.

• • • Black Label Buddha

Perhaps one way to approach the mystery of love that is the guru-disciple relationship is to share some of my own experiences with the Advaita master, Ramesh S. Balsekar. What follows is in the form of stories and vignettes.

I was visiting Ramesh on Maui and had several lengthy conversations with him concerning the guru-disciple relationship. At the end of our time together he was going back to India and would not return to North America again. Already in his seventies, he no longer wanted to be away from his extended family, which included his grandchildren. As we parted he said, "Come and visit me in Bombay. When you've booked tickets give me a call and I'll help you find accommodation."

I had no desire to return to India. I'd been quite ill on my first visit and had no wish to repeat the experience.

As time passed, however, I knew I had to see him again, so I made the necessary arrangements. My friend Brian would accompany me. We were to fly to Bombay from Honolulu via Bangkok. I called Ramesh to tell him I was coming. After giving him the particulars concerning our arrival and length of stay, he asked if I would do him a favor. I hesitated but said I would. "What would you like me to do?" I asked. Ramesh replied, "Would you bring me a large bottle of Black Label?" I was surprised at his request and not completely sure what he meant; after all, this was not what I expected from a guru. He noticed my hesitation. "Is there something wrong?" he inquired. I told him there was nothing wrong. "Do you know what Black Label is?" I said I thought it was a whisky, which he confirmed. Before we hung up he made the same request of Brian.

Not wishing to risk the Black Label in the aircraft cargo hold, Brian and I took the bottles with us in our carry-on luggage, which didn't leave much room. We arrived in Bombay about two in the morning. Once we cleared customs we took a taxi through the deserted streets of the sleeping city to our hotel. Everything was grey and covered in dust, and the unusual fluorescent lights gave the city a feeling of unreality. From time to time we saw people huddled in the gutter around small fires which provided bright sparks of life and color in an otherwise monochrome world. When we arrived at our hotel in Collaba we discovered it was on the fifth floor of an old building. The elevator wasn't running, and on every landing families lay sleeping. There'd been a famine and people from the country had moved to the cities in the hope of eking out a living. We hoisted our bags over those who slept, trying not to disturb them. On the fifth floor we found Precash, the concierge, asleep outside the entrance—something quite normal, it turned out, for that was his bedroom. Sleepy, with tousled hair, Precash helped with our bags and showed us to our room.

In the morning we took a taxi to Ramesh's home, a thirty-minute drive to Gamadia Road in another part of the city. We bought flowers from a flower stand, and started down the hill, hauling the bottles of Black Label with us. Arriving at Ramesh's apartment, we rode an old elevator to the top floor. To our right was a door with Ramesh's name on a brass plate. We knocked, and moments later Ramesh stood before us beaming. He took the flowers and the whisky and handed them to a servant, who vanished into the kitchen and returned moments later with the flowers beautifully arranged in big vases. Ramesh ushered us into his large airy living room and made us welcome. He inquired of our trip, our health and our families. Several minutes later, the servant returned carrying trays of tea and delicate finger foods made by Ramesh's wife, Sharda. We'd arrived early and it was half an hour before a couple more guests were ushered into the room.

During these years there was only a trickle of seekers who sought out the master, and the number of people present at any one time was usually between two and five. Over the next week Brian and I always arrived early and consequently were witness to the numerous people who brought with them gifts of—you guessed it—Black Label! We became curious. Did he have a cellar somewhere, we wondered? Was he selling it? What was going on?

One day, someone asked about it. Ramesh looked up with a mischievous smile and said, "Funny you should ask; my wife's been asking the same question." He paused and we waited. "As you know, I was a bank manager before my retirement, and from time to time some of my friends come by and I like to offer them a good whiskey"—something not available in India at the time. We looked at him but were not convinced. Then with a twinkle in his eyes he said, "I suppose you'd like to know the real reason, wouldn't you?"

"Of course," we agreed.

"When someone is coming from far away to see a guru, it can be, as you know, very expensive. People from the West have preconceived notions; they don't always understand the role of the guru, what he is like, how he behaves, and so on. When I ask people to bring me Black Label, you'd be surprised how many decide not to come. I don't fit the image they have in their minds of a guru.

That image would prevent them from hearing what I have to say. This saves them time and expense."

A couple of days later he mentioned he was having a family gathering the following Wednesday and those of us who were at the talks were invited to attend. Wednesday evening arrived and Ramesh greeted us at the door, dressed in Western attire, slacks and a short-sleeved shirt. His wife Sharda was present, as well as his brother, his son and his wife, and their two children, along with those of us who'd been attending the morning talks. Ramesh was the perfect host. Seating us, he made the introductions and helped us feel at home. He offered us whisky, or whatever we might like. He kept careful watch on our glasses and replenished them when needed. A wide variety of delicious foods had been prepared by Sharda. Ramesh served them and described each dish. What a lovely evening we had with the master. On the way to our room that evening I found tears streaming down my face. I was reminded of Christ washing the feet of the disciples.

... Guru hopping

Another incident comes to mind. An American man in his early sixties came to Bombay to speak with Ramesh. He'd been a diligent seeker for many years. His search had taken him all over the world and he'd finally settled at Muktananda's ashram. But Muktananda had died several years before the man's arrival. Riddled with guilt for coming to see Ramesh, he felt he was unfaithful to the man he considered his guru. A woman who'd been visiting for several days expressed a similar concern. She wanted to go and see Amachi. Ramesh chuckled and told her she was welcome to go and see whomever she wanted. He called it "guru hopping" and obviously took great delight in the term. Ramesh's point was: none of us has free will and consequently we will go wherever we need to go, wherever our destiny takes us. He encouraged us to do whatever we felt inclined to do. He had no concern at all and hoped we wouldn't take it personally as he didn't.

A year passed and I returned to India, and as usual spent my time in Bombay with Ramesh. Before leaving on this particular trip, however, I'd read about Poonja Ji, an Advaita master in Lucknow. I decided to go and see him because I was desperate and he was reputed to have the power to bestow enlightenment on his disciples. At the time I didn't know if this was true but I wanted to find out for myself. It took two days on the Rajasthan Express to Delhi and from there another day and another train to Lucknow. We would stay two days before returning to Delhi and our flight home.

When I told Ramesh I was going to see Poonja Ji, he simply accepted it without reservation and talked with me about what I would need for the trip. He always had concern for those who came to see him, and did everything within his power to make their trip as comfortable and free of problems as possible.

It was late morning when we boarded the train for Delhi. As the train passed beyond the city I became aware of a deep sadness. I didn't want to leave Ramesh; he was where I belonged. An image appeared in my mind of a sailboat that had crossed a wide expanse of ocean driven by a strong wind and had arrived in Bombay. As it entered the harbor the wind died and the sails luffed as the boat came to rest.

As it turned out Poonja Ji was not of any help to me.

• • • The love of the lover for the beloved

One morning I arrived early and sat cross-legged in one of the plush armchairs in the master's spacious living room. Light streamed through the open windows. Two men arrived and Ramesh engaged them in conversation, inquiring what brought them to Bombay and answering their questions. I paid little attention to the conversation, quite content instead to hear the soothing cadence of Ramesh's voice. Outside, the noise of traffic rose from the street, accompanied by the persistent blare of horns and the cries of street vendors. Somewhere a child was crying and a mother was comforting it. Through a window the gray ravens circled in the trembling air. I found myself crying, my heart overflowing with love and a deep appreciation for the miracle of the guru. I looked at Ramesh and he was looking at me, his eyes quiet, and a gentle smile on his face. "It's like the love of the lover for the beloved, isn't it?" He'd described it exactly. When my eyes cleared I saw he'd returned to the conversation with his guests.

Sticking

One of the enjoyable things about attending the talks with Ramesh was meeting the people who inevitably stopped in to see him, and listening to the conversations that would ensue. It was obvious that some who came to see Ramesh were just passing through; they'd heard of him and wanted to stop and see him, much as one would stop to see an interesting site in the vicinity. From time to time, someone would come to see him who was keenly interested in what he had to say; his travels came to an end when he entered Ramesh's presence.

One day we were talking about this phenomenon and Ramesh referred to those whose journey had come to an end as those who would "stick." I asked Ramesh, "Did you know I would stick?" "Yes," he replied. "When?" I asked. "The first time I met you," he responded. I was astounded. The first few times I met Ramesh I assumed he saw so many people he might not remember me, and so out of courtesy I would re-introduce myself to him.

In the earlier years with Ramesh I'd wanted to know if he was the guru I'd set out to find. Over time I'd forgotten about it. Occasionally we corresponded. In one of his letters, at the top of the third page I came across the following words: "My dear Colin I want you to know, that I know you have accepted me as your guru and I take that responsibility seriously." Ramesh's words confirmed what I'd come to know, but never given voice to before. Tears and an unfathomable joy welled to the surface. I felt as if I'd been given the keys to the universe.

• • • Cleverness

My wife accompanied me to India on one of the trips to see Ramesh. One morning Ramesh mentioned that an elderly American was arriving the next day. It was his first time in India and Ramesh asked us to find accommodation for him near our hotel. We found a room a short distance away. In the morning when we arrived at Ramesh's the American was already there. I recognized him at once; his name was Joe.

When Ramesh was on Maui I'd explored in considerable depth the guru-disciple relationship. The room where the talks were taking place was large and there were about forty in attendance. Both Ramesh and I are a bit hard of hearing, and I was sitting toward the back of the hall. Ramesh asked me to come and sit up front so we could hear each other better and wouldn't have to shout.

Toward the end of the talks a number of people stood to express their thanks to Ramesh, to let him know how much they appreciated what he had to say and the clarity he'd brought to them. Joe was one of them. He was emotional and had some difficulty expressing himself through all the tears. As what he said mirrored my own feelings, I felt a sympathetic bond with him.

I was so pleased to see him and happily shook his hand. At the end of the talk we took Joe with us in the taxi and showed him to his room. In the morning we picked him up for the ride to the home of Ramesh. Joe began by asking a question, which I don't remember now. Ramesh responded with a careful and clear explanation. Joe rephrased his question and Ramesh proceeded to answer it again. When he finished Joe asked the same question again from a slightly different perspective. This went on all morning and Ramesh patiently and graciously answered Joe's question.

The next morning the same thing happened; Joe asked his question and Ramesh patiently answered. Those of us present were getting tired of the process, and at times, when Joe voiced his question an audible sigh could be heard in the room. At one point Ramesh got up and in apparent exasperation turned to me and said, "See if you can get through to him," and left the room. I looked at Joe and began to explain what Ramesh had been saying. Joe blew up; he became extremely angry. It was as though I'd just poured gasoline on a hot fire. I immediately stopped talking and waited for Ramesh to return.

The room was silent when Ramesh came back. He

looked at us sitting silently but said nothing. The talks ended shortly afterward. Outside, the three of us got into the taxi. My wife and Joe sat in the back and I in the front. As soon as were seated Joe exploded. "You're so arrogant," he yelled at me. "You think you know it all. You are one of Ramesh's favorites. He had you sit near him when we were on Maui." Knowing Ramesh as I did, I knew he did not consider anyone better or worse than anyone else. We were all equal in his eyes. I was completely taken aback by Joe's angry comments. He continued, "If I'd known you were going to be here I wouldn't have come; you're my worst nightmare." Then turning to my wife he asked, "How can you stand such arrogance?" And, much to my chagrin, she explained how she could. I was very upset with her. After we dropped Joe off at the hotel we went up to our room and got into a heated argument.

In the morning Joe didn't meet us for the ride to Ramesh's, and when we arrived for the talks, he was absent. Ramesh explained that Joe had caught a flight back to the US. I was stunned. Ramesh looked at my wife and asked, "What happened?" I was deeply embarrassed by the whole affair and what she said only seemed to make it worse. I wondered if Ramesh had set me up the day before when he'd told me to try and get through to Joe. Ramesh looked at me and began to talk about "cleverness." I didn't understand him. He said, "Your cleverness gets in the way; it will block enlightenment." I heard the words and was deeply saddened. I really didn't understand what he was talking about. I looked at him and there was nothing but love shining in his eyes. His words, though clear and precise, were soft, and the tone of his voice was one of love and respect. There was not a trace of anger in him, simply a deep flow of compassion. For some reason I could not comprehend what he was saying. It was as if I was in a bell jar and his words simply bounced off. I could hear them clearly; I knew what they meant; but the understanding eluded me.

The next day we were returning to Hawaii, and would go from the talks to catch our plane. That evening I called Ramesh and asked if we could come early in the morning, as I wanted to talk with him more about cleverness. He agreed. In the morning I sat before him and Ramesh explained cleverness to me again. I remember saying to him that the only desire in my heart was to be of help to people and that it had been there all my life. "It's cleverness," he insisted again and again. "You have a good understanding of human nature; you're perceptive and can see into people; but your cleverness gets in the way." Once more I had the sensation of being in a bell jar and his words were simply not entering my mind. It was disconcerting. Ramesh tried to get through to me again. I still didn't get it but I noticed my wife nodding her head.

She was good at explaining things and she obviously understood what Ramesh was saying. Not wanting to waste Ramesh's time and interrupt the talks, I told him,

"She understands; she can explain it to me." Ramesh nodded his head and the subject was changed. The whole event shook me a great deal, and when I said goodbye to Ramesh it was with a sad heart.

A month later, my wife asked if I was ready to hear what Ramesh was trying to tell me in Bombay. I felt a jolt go through me. "Ramesh said that you have understood the teachings, you have insight and can easily understand people, and that's what makes you a good psychologist. But, when he spoke of cleverness, what he meant is what I mean when I talk about you getting on your soap box." I began to feel the same deep embarrassment sweep over me. She continued, "When people come to see you, seeking help in your role as a psychologist, they are asking for your help. Then you must respond to their request and give them what they need. Sometimes you go outside your professional role, trying to help when your help has not been asked for. This is offensive. If a couple get into a fight at a social gathering, you try and help them to resolve their differences. They are not asking for your help, and as a result they resent your intrusion. You explain away the hostility directed at you by thinking them ungrateful."

I understood. What she said was true. The embarrassment deepened and I felt it for days. I wrote to Ramesh and described what my wife had explained. He responded, "What she said is accurate. She has stated it clearly and much better than I was able to."

In my letter I'd asked, "What can I do to stop this behavior?" His response I was deeply familiar with. "My dear Colin, there's nothing you can do about this, it is simply not in your hands. All you can do, perhaps, is to watch it; and in time, if you're lucky, it will pass."

For months I watched my unwanted behavior. I hated it, and found it sickening. It just kept happening, however, and wouldn't stop. I'd no idea how prevalent it was in my life. I began to notice that in situations where it happened there was a great deal of physical tension in my body. Life became deeply discordant; this was intolerable for me. I saw how much of life I could not accept; I could not allow it to remain as it was in what I considered its broken and dysfunctional form. I found myself almost rocking onto my toes, reaching to solve the dysfunction.

For almost a year the behavior continued. I thought it would never end. One day an event took place, I saw it and felt the tension subside. Things were fine the way they were, nothing needed to be done. I could accept whatever was happening without the compulsion to fix it. As the days passed I could feel the accumulated tension draining out of my body.

From time to time the old behavior happened, but less and less. Sometimes the thought would enter my mind to try and resolve a situation, and then I could feel the impulse subside. What a relief! Life and the people in it were fine exactly as they were, and so was I. There was no need to help, unless asked.

I'd been traveling for several months and found myself at a gathering in the mountains, a kind of festival for humanity. I had books displayed on a table and had gone to lunch. When I returned a rather diminutive man sat at the table reading. I took a seat and he continued to read. When he finished he looked up and in a deep booming voice asked a question. Instantly the answer came out of my mouth, before I could think of it. Late in the day I left and drove higher into the mountains, further and further away from people. Sometime later I had occasion to speak with Ramesh and I described what happened. "You have a good understanding of the teachings; you must answer people's questions, when they ask," he ordered in no uncertain terms. "To refuse to do so is as much the function of the ego as cleverness."

Cleverness as used by Ramesh in this instance is really the same as the idea of "hubris" referred to earlier as the "Unforgivable Sin" or "the Sin Against the Holy Spirit."

The fragrance of the master

I lived for a couple of months in the mountains east of San Diego. I'd been thinking about Ramesh and wishing I could go and talk with him. But a trip to India at the time was out of the question. I'd been traveling in the mainland US in an attempt to market one of my books. I spent a great deal of time alone. Occasionally

I wouldn't speak with anyone for weeks at a time. No wonder I wasn't successful at marketing the book! One day I found myself thinking about certain aspects of the teaching which I'd discussed with Ramesh on the last trip to India.

That evening I went for a long walk along a trail threading a stand of old oak trees that provided welcome shade and relief from the intense heat. The sun was about to set and I found myself pondering a statement Ramesh had made. I was recalling the last trip to India. We'd been talking about how difficult it was to come and see him and the times I felt the strong need to be in his presence. As we were about to leave he said, "I am with you always." Instantly I recognized Christ's statement to his disciples.

Ramesh was never out of my thoughts. He'd taken up residence in my heart, a continuing and peaceful presence that pervaded life, like a subtle and gentle fragrance. Upon returning from my walk the sun slipped beneath the horizon and darkness gathered under the trees. Climbing into the camper, my home away from home, I made a cup of tea and read for a while before going to bed. The question I'd been pondering for days was still unresolved.

During the night, Ramesh appeared to me in what must have been a dream. We talked and in his usual thorough way cleared up the difficulty I'd been having. I was so glad to see him. He was absolutely radiant. I soaked all night in his presence. In the morning when I woke up I could still feel that presence. I washed and dressed and went for a walk across some open hills dotted with oak trees. The morning sun cast long shadows and dew sparkled in the tall grass where cobwebs hung between them. Tears streamed down my face. It was mid-morning when Ramesh and I returned to the camper. He spent several days with me in the mountains outside San Diego.

Later, when I returned to India, I told Ramesh of my experience and asked if he was aware of what happened. He never commented, simply smiled his usual smile; but did I detect, or did I project, that twinkle in his eyes?

• • • The cobra strikes

On the last trip to India I arrived outside Ramesh's apartment to find a crowd of a hundred or more people waiting to enter. In the years since my previous visit, he'd become well known, and many Westerners now attended the talks. A considerable number of Osho sanyasins came from Poona.

When new people arrived, Ramesh would inquire what brought them to see him and what they had understood so far. On one particular morning a young German arrived from Poona. A disciple of Osho, he'd begun teaching. From his comments it was clear he considered himself enlightened and proud of it. He understood the language but it was obvious to most of us he had a huge ego. Ramesh tried to engage him in dialogue but he was cagey and full of himself. Arrogantly he challenged Ramesh and ridiculed what he had to say. Ramesh was a small man, hardly five feet tall. I sensed something shift in him. The internal image was of a cobra suddenly poised, its hood extended, and ready to strike. The exchange was swift and to the point. In all the years I'd been with Ramesh I'd never seen him attack as he did at that moment. He was completely respectful of the young man but his words punctured the pretension for all to see. The exchange lasted no more than a couple of minutes, but in that short time Ramesh exposed the man's ego. The young man left severely shaken and did not return. As he left I sensed the cobra relax and its hood pull back.

Several days passed, and shortly after Ramesh began speaking, a note was handed to him; Ramesh read it aloud. The young man in question was downstairs and requesting permission to come and attend the talks. At once he was welcomed. What a change had taken place! The arrogance was gone, replaced by a vulnerable openness and newfound respect for the master. Ramesh explained he was always welcome to attend the talks and didn't need permission; all were welcome. He then went on to say it was perfectly legitimate for anyone who came to see him to challenge him; to test him, so to speak, to be sure that enlightenment had taken place; and he was thus authorized to speak. What was not acceptable was to ask a question and not listen to the response.

••• Frank

I'd just returned from a three-month trip to India when one morning I received an unexpected call. "My name is Frank," the caller said, by way of introduction, "I'm a friend of Ramesh." After a few moments he explained the purpose of his call. He was a retired professor from the University of California in San Diego. Ramesh, as it turned out, was his guru, although he never referred to Ramesh in that way. "European and some American universities have a tradition that when a beloved professor becomes elderly they compile a book of letters and articles by his students explaining the impact his teaching had in their lives. The book is called a Festschrift, and is given as a gift to the professor in appreciation for his contribution to their lives." As it turns out Frank had obtained permission from Ramesh to compile a Festschrift in his honor. Frank, however, had a heart attack and could not begin the project. He asked Ramesh if he knew a writer who could take over for him and Ramesh had given him my name.

I was thrilled to be selected by Ramesh and for the next two years I talked with and corresponded with many of Ramesh's disciples, obtaining their stories. In April of 1996 the book was published. In it is one of the most moving accounts of awakening I ever came across; an awakening that involved Frank in a profound and intimate way. As it turns out Frank had become enlightened too, several years earlier.

During one of my visits to India I had spoken with Ramesh about Frank, at which time he confirmed Frank's enlightenment. He went on to explain, however, that Frank did not believe enlightenment had taken place. When I asked how this could be, Ramesh simply shrugged. He didn't know.

In the summer of 1996 I was in San Diego and went to see Frank. Then, over a period of nine months I visited him from time to time. I thoroughly enjoyed being with him; he was always kind and gracious. In conversations with him about enlightenment he mentioned that he didn't think enlightenment had happened in his case, although, he acknowledged, Ramesh thought otherwise.

I have often puzzled over this strange phenomenon. For myself, however, it was clear that Frank was indeed enlightened. Being in his presence was like being in Ramesh's presence. Not a trace of ego was anywhere present. Perhaps it had to do with his unassuming nature; that is, when the change took place it was virtually indiscernible.

• • • Is the guru necessary?

In the shamanic tradition the role of the "man of knowledge" is clear. It is his task to assist the neophyte to penetrate the illusion of life by breaking open the underlying unexamined assumptions concerning the acculturation process. From the perspective of the shamanic tradition it was understood that each human being was surrounded by a cocoon of energy and at a particular location within the cocoon was a focal point—much like the slider on a metronome that determines a particular beat—the placement of which determined the general description of the world he saw. The shaman's job was to shift that point by questioning what was taken for granted, those unexamined assumptions and agreements about which we are largely ignorant. He did this from outside the neophyte's limited world view.

The guru serves a similar function. The guru's task is to awaken the seeker from the sleep of illusion. What is difficult about this task is that the sleep of life bears great similarity to the actual awakened state: consider the following scenario.

There's a large room full of people at a social gathering. The room is well appointed with comfortable chairs and plush carpets. In the middle is a large glass coffee table, its edges pointed and sharp. People are deeply engaged in conversation but every now and then someone walks into the coffee table and lets out a cry of pain. It is observed that many of those present do the same thing; walk into the coffee table. Looking more carefully it is possible to see that large numbers of those present are limping, and blood can be seen seeping through their clothes from injured shins.

Why do people walk into the table? They have their eyes open, so how come they don't avoid it? To the observer's astonishment some of the people who've already walked into the table do so again and sometimes even a third or fourth time. Why do they not see what they're doing? The answer is simple; they are sleepwalkers. Amongst them, however, there are some who are not sleepwalkers; some in the room are actually awake. How do we tell them apart, though? As we continue to observe, it becomes clear that a few of those present don't walk into the table more than once. Instead they pay attention; once is enough. A peculiar thing begins to happen. One of the sleepwalkers is moving toward the table when one of the awakened ones intercepts him and shakes him, trying to wake him. The sleepwalker becomes aggressive and pushes the awakened one away. To try and wake up the sleeper can be dangerous until the pain of his injuries brings him to the edge of wakefulness. The deaths of Socrates and Christ are examples of just how dangerous this role can be.

The guru's role is to assist the seeker in waking up. The guru does this by drawing attention to the truth, that which the seeker already knows. He does this by various means designed to tickle into awareness what the seeker has always known.

A Zen story illustrates this very well. A man was fishing and caught a fish but the fish was too small so he threw it back in the water. For the first time the fish realized it had been swimming in something.

I used to work for a magician. One thing I learned from those days was that it was easy to trap a person's attention by doing something glaringly obvious, something about which he was curious; and while the attention was thus engaged one could do something else in plain view and it would not be noticed. What appears to be magic is nothing more than capturing a person's attention and redirecting it without his knowledge. Life is an amazing magic show. The guru's job is to shift the awareness from illusion to reality. As the young chick seeks to break out of the egg from the inside, the guru like the mother hen seeks to break the egg from the outside.

So, is the guru essential to the awakening process? Not always, but in most instances, the answer is yes. Examples of spontaneous unassisted awakenings are rare. The only one with which I'm familiar is that of Ramana Maharshi. That's not to say that life experiences don't have a powerful effect on the process that leads to awakening; but the actual event of enlightenment itself tends to require the presence of the guru at some stage. This is not something most Westerners like to hear. Remember, this is a description, however, simply factual information.

··· False gurus

In the West physicians play a role in society that used to be held in high regard. Amongst them there are those who've entered the field for purely monetary reasons; they are in fact less like physicians and more like avaricious business men. There are physicians who have technical and intellectual knowledge but lack intuitive insight and may not be keen observers. Some physicians are out-and-out charlatans, interested only in power and guided completely by self-interest, too often at the expense of their clients.

There are however, some who are born healers. Healing is rooted deep within them; it is in their very fiber; it is their dharma. These healers are genuine and their function is that of pure service; they care deeply about the well-being of people. In the East they'd be called karma yogis. The fact that some physicians are not true healers has no bearing on the effectiveness of the true healer.

The same can be said of the guru. In cultures like India and Japan, where the guru, the true spiritual teacher, has an accepted role to play, the same holds true. Amongst them are those with an incomplete understanding, those who are charlatans, those who are interested in power and exploitation; and, there are genuine masters, whose dharma is to facilitate the awakening process in those who seek them out.

When self-interest operates in the guru, when he seeks to control his disciples or to hang onto them, and when he prescribes behavior or a set of beliefs, he would be considered a false guru. My own experience was that after hearing about Ramesh, I read some of what he'd written. In particular I was able to read correspondence between him and his disciples. As I read, it seemed clear he knew what he was talking about; and his manner and attitude were relaxed, without pretense and accompanied by a quiet, simple humility—not the kind of thing that can be deliberately practiced.

When I went to see him I still had some skepticism, but the more I was around him the more relaxed, open and receptive I became. Ramesh answered all my questions. All questions were legitimate; there were no wrong questions or questions that could not or should not be asked. Months passed, and one day I realized I had absolutely no doubt about him; I trusted him implicitly. I listened carefully to his responses, and accepted that what he said was the truth even before I understood it fully. As a result, over time, that which obscured understanding slowly faded, revealing that to which his words pointed.

... Believe it or not

There are many documented accounts of gurus possessing considerable powers. For instance, Ram Das's guru, Maharaji—Neem Karoli Baba—possessed great powers, powers most ordinary people haven't developed. He knew where to find his disciples and when they would be in a particular location. At times he would travel by train and at others he simply appeared, having traversed a great distance in a very short time. He also appears to have had the capacity to know what was going to happen before it did. Often when he traveled by train, conductors who knew him wouldn't take any money from him, as they loved to have him on board and considered it a blessing. One day, however, a conductor was rude to him and threw him off the train. When the train started to leave it couldn't move. No matter what the engineers did, it seemed to be incapable of moving. It didn't move until the conductor apologized to Maharaji and invited him back on the train. Everything he did was for others, either in a straightforward manner or as a means of bringing home some aspect of his teaching, as in the situation with the arrogant conductor who needed to learn humility.

Sai Baba is reputed to have considerable powers as well. While at his ashram in the winter of 1990 I saw vibhutti, a sacred ash, appear from the palm of his hand and land in the palm of a friend with whom I was traveling. I also spoke at great length to a man and his wife who lived at the ashram. Both were elderly; the man was a retired army officer of high rank. His wife described the man's death several years earlier. Shortly after his death Sai Baba restored his life. This reminded me of the reports cited in the New Testament of Christ's ability to raise the dead.

Sai Baba believes education to be important and has created schools all over India. While at the ashram he invited a class of students to attend and presented them with awards. One student had done particularly well. Sai Baba moved his hand in a circular motion palm down, and then suddenly turning the palm up he flipped it away from him. Immediately a gold medallion appeared with a gold chain, which he caught with one of his fingers; he then placed the medallion around the student's neck.

While traveling to southern India we stopped at an orphanage sponsored by Sai Baba. On a large photograph of the master, vibhutti had spontaneously appeared. For years the ash built up and fell from the photograph to the floor where it accumulated. I'd heard of this happening at different places throughout India but this was the first time I had seen it.

Once more, these stories are reminiscent of similar descriptions of Christ's power: turning water into wine and feeding the five thousand.

For the spiritual seeker who hears these stories, it would be easy to assume that enlightenment brought with it such powers, but that is not the case. Neither Jean Klein nor Ramesh ever exhibited such powers, and they quite openly stated they did not have them. The same appears to be true of Ramana Maharshi. Let me digress for a moment, with a story I'd like to share about Ramana. It took place when he was in his later years, and it demonstrates the real magic of love.

Darshan means to be in the presence of the master. Ramana would hold darshan in the morning and evening. Summers at the ashram were hot, and winters cold. One of his disciples was an elderly woman he called Ma. Ma suffered from severe arthritis but she loved Ramana more than anything or anyone else in the world. In warm weather she would always attend darshan, but when it was particularly cold in the winter she was confined to her bed.

Ramana always brushed his teeth near a rock at the back of the ashram. During his life the only clothing he ever wore was a loin cloth, so when he went to clean his teeth in the winter it was very cold. Some of his disciples tried to discourage the practice but Ramana would not be dissuaded. They offered to heat water and bring it to him in the hall but he refused. When spring returned Ma came with it. One of her fellow disciples greeted her, glad to see her again. "I'm sorry you've had to miss darshan over the winter," he said to her. "Oh, but I didn't," she replied. "The room with my bed looks over the ashram grounds and I had darshan with Ramana every morning when he cleaned his teeth. When he was finished he always looked my way and smiled."

Back to the topic at hand. In India psychic or unusual powers are referred to as "Siddhis." From the perspective of Jnanna Yoga, Siddhis are considered a trap for the seeker and are not encouraged or given any importance. The reason for this is that they have nothing to do with the process of spiritual awakening. In fact, they can be a serious impediment to the process. Why? The ego is easily inflated, as we all know. Think about it. We buy a new car, someone tells us what a great car we've bought, and we immediately take it as a reflection on ourselves. As spiritual seekers, however, we don't need anything to be proud of; we don't need anything to inflate the ego, because it is only when the ego dies that awakening takes place.

Obviously some masters do possess Siddhis and use them in effective ways. For the true master the ego has already died and so there's no concern he will take pride in the unusual power he possesses.

In the pursuit of knowledge
More and more is accumulated.
In the pursuit of the Tao
More and more falls away.

Lao Tzu

Chapter 19

Satsang, what it is and how it works.

The word satsang comes from sanskrit and means to be in the presence of the master, literally to breath the same air or share the same space as the master.

Satsang is a different process from that of learning as understood in the West. From a Western perspective knowledge is acquired. One of the predominant requirements in the acquisition of knowledge is a good memory. Satsang's purpose, however, is quite different. It seeks to bring forth the understanding inherent in all of us, which in fact does not require memory. That is why learned knowledge can be forgotten whereas understanding, when it happens, is permanent. It cannot be undone once it has taken place. This is an important distinction.

Another difference between learning and understanding is that in learning the student tends to emulate the teacher's methods whereas with understanding the methods are irrelevant. This is why what Ramesh taught appears in many ways so different from the teachings of his guru, Nissargadatta. The same goes for Ramesh's enlightened disciples. This explains why masters speak with authority from a deeply shared understanding while using different stories, techniques; even philosophical contexts.

Some refer to Advaita Vedanta as a philosophy. But, strictly speaking it is not. If it was it could be learned. But, Advaita cannot be learned. What Advaita actually is, is a description of reality with an invitation, in fact, a requirement that the student find out for himself if what the master points to is true. This is not something that generally happens overnight. Why? Because the process of separating reality from belief is not an easy one. It is, however, essential for real understanding to take place.

As was mentioned earlier there is a distinction between the role of the teacher and the role of the guru. The teacher's role is to facilitate the learning process, the accumulation of knowledge, whereas the guru's role is to facilitate unlearning. It turns out that the dismantling of beliefs reveals the simple reality obscured by them.

In addition to the use of language and intellect in satsang there is another more subtle process taking place. Some gurus, Ramana Maharshi for instance, were said to teach in silence. From a Western perspective this process might be called entrainment, which can be said to take place all the time when in the presence of the master, whether in silence or not. (see http://en.wikipedia.org/wiki/Entrainment_(physics))

The idea of entrainment is best understood from the perspective of energy. A calm and peaceful energy tends to bring forth a similar peacefulness in those whose energy is disturbed.

When the strings of a guitar are tuned to a particular key they are also tuned to each other. When slightly off key there is a harmonic distortion audible to the ear. As the strings harmonize with each other the dissonance disappears. It could be said that harmony is a natural and steady state and all disturbance moves toward it.

Satsang, as practiced in the East, has been passed down from generation to generation over thousands of years. Because the tradition has largely been lost in the West, we who grew up here have some difficulty understanding its purpose and how it works. We tend to think of satsang as a kind of discussion group amongst friends and fellow seekers. But this is not the case. Satsang is a process which leads to the removal of that which stands in the way of direct understanding, our beliefs.

The master is that, a master. His task is to bring the light of awareness to the student/disciple; awareness of those things he may have taken for granted, or those things about which he is deeply unaware. There comes a time for some seekers when they actively look for someone who can answer their questions.

Having already done considerable research, the seeker is keenly aware he has not found what he's looking for. He may have gone to those considered authorities only to find they knew no more than he did.

What seekers want is the peace the master has. By now they have little interest in discussion with other seekers when in the presence of the master. They might even feel impatient with those who think of satsang as a discussion group and interrupt the flow of dialogue between the master and the seeker.

Satsang is not a discussion group. It is a process of deep inquiry where questions are directed to the master and close attention paid to the responses. It may be noted at times that the same question raised by different people brings forth different responses. This is important as the master is often responding to a deeper question hidden in the words.

Does this mean that there's no time or place when seekers may discuss amongst themselves the process in which they are deeply involved? No, it does not mean this. What it does mean is that satsang is not the place for it.

During the twenty years I went to India and met Ramesh and fellow disciples there was no discussion amongst ourselves during satsang. Afterwards, however, we had lively and informative discussions; usually in small intimate groups of friends and acquaintances from all over the world. This often took place over lunch after leaving Ramesh. Sometimes we explored together the environs of Mumbai and a culture and land so different from our own.

These groups changed constantly as new people arrived and others left. Many friendships were formed and in lengthy discussions with friends we were able to formulate deeper and more precise questions to ask Ramesh.

When missionaries arrived in Hawaii
they discovered a people with no concept of sin.
The idea of salvation meant nothing to them:
salvation from what, for what?

Chapter 20

Further Observations On Understanding

Points of view

As time passed and the understanding deepened, I noticed something unusual taking place in conflict situations; these involved a number of different people with strong and opposing positions. When I listened carefully I could understand someone's position completely. Then I would listen to someone else and the same thing happened. I could understand their position and their point of view, and I certainly couldn't fault them for their perspective. In listening to another person, the same thing took place. There might be a severe difference of opinions, and yet when I listened closely and came to understand, I noticed I had no judgment, simply insight into all the positions taken. It was clear there was no right or wrong about anything, no one person who was right and no one who was wrong.

Although Che Guevera and Fidel Castro were hated by many Americans, when understood they could not be faulted, as many of their motives were noble. The same can be said about such people as Osama bin Laden, and George Bush. This may not be a popular perspective given current concern over issues of terrorism and American foreign policy, for instance, but it is the one approach that can yield constructive results when it comes to resolving conflict. To see someone as evil, as simply victimizing people without cause, does not help. It is nothing other than the projection of the ego, whose tendency is to divide the world into good and bad and thus to impose on life something not there naturally.

When my son was about nine he came home from school one day in a terrible state. He'd been crying and had bruises on his face and cuts on his arms. I thought he'd been in an accident. It was no accident—he'd been set upon by four boys who lived a mile down the street. I was very angry over what they'd done. Somehow I had the wisdom to know this was important and had to be handled carefully. Derick and I drove to where the boys lived. I knocked on four doors and fortunately each of the boys appeared. They were obviously scared but somehow I convinced them I wasn't going to hurt them. The six of us sat on the lawn in a circle. I told them I wanted to get to the bottom of what happened and to do that I asked that each of them describe what had taken place from his perspective. I got them to agree to listen and not interrupt the person speaking. Then we went around the circle and each boy described what had happened. All the accounts were different, and the five boys listened attentively to each other. There were some things that weren't clear, so I posed questions and got the boys to respond to them. I was so focused on what was happening with the boys, I'd not at first noticed that some parents and adults had gathered around listening. Each of the boys had as much time as they needed to speak, and by the end of our time together there was nothing left to say that had not already been said. All the buckets were empty, so to speak. Since all of us had listened carefully, understanding came about; it was an understanding that encompassed the whole, and all those present shared that understanding. The issue of right and wrong did not play a part. What was immensely gratifying was that my son was not beaten up again, and the boys got along afterwards.

When we're asleep, unaware of our behavior and its effects, no change takes place. Once the awakening process begins, we might become aware of our negative behavior. Perhaps the awareness results from someone pointing it out, or because of the suffering it causes, or simply as a result of dispassionate observation, or all three. At first the behavior will happen and we won't notice it; then a month later, we remember what happened, and suddenly we see what we did. Then the behavior happens again and this time a week passes before we see it. Then a day will pass, an hour, a minute, moments, and then we will see it at the time it happens. Then one glorious day, the thought arises that gives birth to the behavior in the first place, and it is simply witnessed and no action follows. The unwanted behavior has died, and just as direct sunlight dispels shadow, awareness dispels the unwanted behavior.

• • • Thoughts on bondage, sin and religion

The spiritual seeker is not content with life; he wants more. He has a disease that Ralph Waldo Emerson called "divine discontent." The seeker believes he's not free. He doesn't know what freedom is but he's convinced he doesn't have it. In the language used to describe spiritual awakening, this feeling of not being free is known as "bondage." By and large, most people are relatively content with their lives, content to make a living and raise a family, go to movies, have picnics and take in a parade. The spiritual seeker can do all these things too, but remains deeply dissatisfied, and it is the deep dissatisfaction that drives him to uncover the mystery of life; to become enlightened or to find God. Without the sense of being in bondage, the spiritual search does not take place. Although I dislike the Christian idea of sin, it does perhaps serve, in a vivid way, the same purpose as the concept of bondage. This idea is clearly visible in the historic encounter between the Hawaiian people and the Christian missionaries.

When the missionaries first arrived in Hawaii they discovered a people who had no concept of sin. As a result the idea of salvation meant nothing to them; salvation from what, for what? The missionaries, creative people that they were, embarked upon a full-fledged campaign to teach the Hawaiians they were sinners, further claiming that the plagues and diseases that decimated the Hawaiian people (deliberately caused in some instances) were of course the inevitable result of sin.

Ignorance and arrogance still masquerade as religion and continue in various forms today. In extreme cases it can advocate, for instance, the use of suicide bombers, as a means of destroying the infidel and thereby doing one's sacred duty. Or it might take the form of state sponsored land theft and the building of settlements as in Palestine. A less virulent form is evident in the New Age Movement where illness, accidents and apparent failures are attributed to a lack of "clear intention." A lack of clear intention is, of course, the new sin, the new bondage.

Yet, this is all part of life, part of the dream, created by the Source, the same source that brings understanding. When awakening takes place, the ignorance that gives rise to such practices dissolves, like a shadow which fades in the light.

Perfect yet mysteriously formed
It existed before time ever was.

It is the silent void
Eternally present
Solitary and unchanging.

It is the Great Mother of the universe
And, for want of a better word
We call it the Tao.

Lao Tzu

Chapter 21

The Dance Of Life

Entertainment

Life is an intricate and intimate dance—what the Hindu refers to as "God's Lila." There's the dance of electrons in the material world. There's the dance of light off water, of wind through trees and across the hills; the dance of snowflakes, and even the complex dance of the ego on the world stage. Truly all of life is a dance.

Human beings sometimes wonder why life came about. The question cannot really be answered, but for those who insist on an answer anyway . . . Why not? Put in more theological terms the questions is posed, "Why did God create the universe?" Not to be trite, but is not the answer, "For something to do?" After all, God as the supreme potential must become active, and in such activation the world of form is born. Another answer to this question is that God created the universe for entertainment. A definition of entertainment is: Something, especially a performance, that beguiles or holds one's attention. Life certainly beguiles us and holds our attention. It is held by the awesome beauty that comprises the great mystery, and by the drama played out on the world stage, the ego's drama.

In the Sermon on the Mount, Christ says, "Blessed are the peacemakers, for they shall inherit the earth." He could just as easily have said, "Blessed are the war makers, for they give the peacemakers something to do."

When I first started working in the field of psychology, it was obvious I'd have no job if it weren't for the fact that human beings sometimes have problems. Consequently I was appreciative and respectful, because clients were the other part of the cosmic equation. The same holds true for the social worker, the physician, the detective and so on. As in the field of psychology, there were some who had little awareness of this fact and arrogantly went about their careers treating other people's problems, families and bodies as their own private playground.

From the perspective of the impersonal consciousness, everything simply is, and there's no problem; one finds oneself doing spontaneously whatever there is to do. When the personal or identified consciousness arises, we have "inter-personal" relationships taking place; and with interpersonal relationships, conflict, intrigue and melodrama abound. There's nothing wrong with this. It is simply the way it is, simply the nature of the personal consciousness, the ego, which is designed to function like this. Without it there'd be no gainful employment for many of us. This is God's dance, the Lila that comprises life; and in the final analysis it makes for fine entertainment.

I once had a conversation with Ramesh about this. Knowing I was a writer he asked what would happen if I wrote a novel in which there were no good guys and no bad guys, no problems, no conflicts, and every thing always worked out as the protagonists hoped. The answer is obvious. The novel would not make the best-seller list and, in fact, it would never be published. Why? We are entertained by conflict, problems and melodrama; it is simply the nature of things; and as such, nothing is wrong. Yet for those who seek permanent peace of mind, melodrama and conflict will not provide it, and we'd be foolish to expect otherwise.

• • • The process of awakening

What is the source of the ego? Metaphorically speaking, it would have to be God, would it not? Furthermore, because there's no free will, there's nothing we can do to bring about the ego's annihilation. As Ramesh says, the ego is not about to commit suicide. It follows, then, that only God, so to speak, can remove the ego. If we try to eliminate or resist the ego we only draw attention to it, and it becomes stronger. All that can be done is to watch what happens; the events taking place, the reactions of ourselves and others to those events, as well as thoughts, which drift through the mind like clouds crossing an empty sky. Having heard the words of the master and having recognized the truth of what he says, there's a certain level of comfort that comes from this understanding. Then as awakening takes place we might observe the shift that happens, a movement from an ego-centered perspective to an impersonal one.

To begin with, the ego's perspective dominates consciousness; but over time, a shift occurs. Imagine standing in a small boat about to step onto the dock. When we place a foot on the dock most of the weight is still in the boat. Once the foot is properly positioned there's a transfer of weight from the boat to the dock. At one point there's more weight on the dock than in the boat and then the complete transfer happens quickly. Awakening can be like that.

At the beginning of the process the change in direction, so to speak, appears minute but quickly becomes dramatic as it diverges from the consensus all around. We are obviously "insane!" At these times I found that listening to the words of Ramesh and reading his books was immensely helpful. Once the weight was more on the dock than in the boat, however, I found I could not read or listen to him anymore, other than to hear the sweet undulating sound of his voice.

Briefly hold a match to paper and it won't ignite. Hold the match longer, the paper begins to burn but it will still go out. Sufficient heat must be generated to create a self-sustaining burn. This is, in short, the process of awakening. It is this process that needs the support of the guru, who fans the flames of realization until they burn by themselves.

In the beginning

Many are familiar with the creation story in Genesis. It starts as follows: "In the beginning God created the heaven and the earth. And the earth was without form, and void; and darkness was upon the face of the deep. And the Spirit of God moved upon the face of the waters."

The moment the spirit of God moved, duality happened and the world of form was born. If it had remained unmoving and dark, there would have been no phenomenal world. The creation story was followed by the story of the Garden of Eden, where man was told not to eat from the tree of the knowledge of good and evil. Curiosity and the nascent ego ensured that God would not be obeyed, and man would know conceptual duality: the knowledge of good and evil.

In the Gospel of John the story is expressed differently: "In the beginning was the Word, and the Word was with God, and the Word was God. The same was in the beginning with God. All things were made through him. Without him was not anything made that has been made. In him was life, and the life was the light of men."

The human being, made in the image and likeness of God, is a creator. When we look about we see the creativity of man everywhere: cell phones, computers, bulldozers, cathedrals, telescopes, and electron microscopes, all examples of the creative capacity of man. Each invention was first of all a thought, a concept, a word. God, being the original creator, had the original idea, and in an instant formulated the concept, and like a voice out of silence, form comes into existence. The same idea is found in Taoism, as Lao Tzu states "silence is the source of all sound."

The creation stories are really metaphors, ways of speaking meant to facilitate understanding. They are not meant to be taken literally. First of all, God is simply a concept. There really is no God, as such, at least in the way human beings conceive of God. The concept of God is just that, a convenient concept with which to speak or contemplate the nature of life, the origin of the universe and other such topics of ultimate concern. (It is a ridiculous concept, though, when it comes to discussions pertaining to whose concept of God is right; but that's another story.)

There are many creation stories, all of which attempt to explain the inexplicable riddle of how the universe and life began. One of the most current stories is the Big Bang Theory, which extrapolates that the universe began from an extremely dense concentration of gases some 13.7 billion years ago. Fred Hoyle, the noted British astronomer, had earlier suggested the universe was constantly being created out of nothing, but his ideas were rejected in favor of the Big Bang Theory. Fred Hoyle had, however, raised an important point, which the Big Bang Theory does not address. Creation out of nothing was considered unscientific; yet the Big Bang Theory is really no better. Where does the cloud of extremely hot and dense gases, the supposed source of the cosmic explosion, come from? There's no answer to this. We keep looking in the phenomenal world for the first cause, the "unmoved mover." The phenomenal world is simply an effect, an appearance of the unseen. In the end, all creation stories are simply attempts to approach the great mystery of life from which we are derived and in which we find ourselves.

Earlier we spoke of how the concept of suffering in life is resolved with the understanding that life is simply a dream—a cosmic one, but a dream nonetheless. It so happens that the idea of the dream also explains the origin of life and of the universe. There's a concept in philosophy known as the noumenal. Noumenal refers to the potential; phenomenal refers to the actual, the world of form. For there to be potential there must also be the actual, or phenomenal. In a sense this is the original duality we spoke of earlier. Without the possibility of something being actualized, potential means nothing.

Once more, what we're describing is the same basic observation found in quantum physics. At the moment consciousness is brought to bear, the potential becomes actual, and creation takes place. This is the real Big Bang.

The origin of the universe, from the perspective of the Big Bang Theory, took place 13.7 billion years ago; but what we've not understood is that the origin of life takes place in the moment that Consciousness dreams the universe into existence. In that moment of dreaming even the 13.7 billion years come into being. As was mentioned, in our dreams there are rivers and mountains millions of years old, and they come into existence, fairly dripping with age, born the moment the dream commences.

How did God dream the universe into existence? Did it happen in time? When did it happen? Was it 13.7 billion years ago? To understand the answer to these questions the reader must be rigorous in his approach, distinguishing between what he knows from firsthand experience and what he believes based on secondhand information, what others have told him. Consider the following illustration.

Reaching for the alarm, you shut it off. The sound of the buzzer has awakened you from a sound sleep. You lie there for a few minutes thinking of the day ahead. You and your wife are going with a friend, Mike, to the top of a nearby glacier and returning two days later. After you've showered you return to the bedroom and gently shake your wife. "Time to get up," you whisper. Two hours later, light suffuses the eastern skyline as you unload the truck and check the equipment one last time. Soon you hoist your packs and begin the climb into the back country. The gloom of the forest gives way to the subdued light of early morning beneath a canopy of fir, hemlock and cedar. You climb steadily. At mid-morning you take a break in a glade beneath a giant cedar. Oregon Junkos twitter in the high branches. The smell of cedar permeates the air, a shaft of sunlight illuminates your resting place and close by the loud cry of a raven can be heard.

By early afternoon you emerge above the tree-line and stop for a rest. The last two hours involved climbing up and down steep inclines. Mike, an avid mountaineer, is your guide for the trip. Dropping the packs, you sit down and share some dates and nuts and take long swigs of water. The black flies are attacking in swarms so the respite is brief. Underway again, you crest a snow-covered ridge and head north. The hot sun has melted the surface, turning it into a slippery sheet of ice. In places it is thick enough to hold your weight, while in others you break through into the deeper snow beneath. It makes for hard going, and already muscles are tired and trembling from the exertion. To the east is a narrow canyon about three thousand feet deep. The other side of the canyon forms a solid rock wall extending five hundred feet above your heads and above which snow ravines provide access to the back of the glacier. These ravines are reached by a narrow intersecting ice-covered ridge that joins the one you're currently traversing about a mile further north. To the west the high plateau is covered with large rocks, snow shadows, stunted trees and glistening pools where blue sky and white clouds are mirrored.

Mike is in the lead, followed by your wife, while you bring up the rear. Mike has insisted that you take out the ice axes in case you slip. Making your way along the ridge, you wonder if you have enough strength to climb the back of the glacier. Your legs are very tired. Suddenly, your wife slips on the icy surface and goes down, sliding toward the canyon edge. She drives her axe deep into the icy surface and stops her slide. Mike spins around to see what's happening. You drive your pick into the ice surface as an anchor and slowly work your way toward her. When you finally reach her she is trembling from fear and exertion. Mike throws you a rope which he's secured around his waist. You lunge for it, and as you do there's a loud crack and the ice on the side of the ridge breaks loose. Everything starts to move, and both of you are moving down the slope. Your wife's eyes are locked on yours; you're both going over the edge and there's nothing you can do. It is three thousand feet to the bottom. You let out a scream—but something is wrong, you hear just a whimper. You claw madly at the surface and at the same moment are launched into space. Instantly you're in another world. You're at home, safe and in bed. You're looking at your wife who's now awake, startled by your thrashing arms. What a relief. It was so real. You thought you were both going to die, and it turned out to be just a dream.

What happened here? You had gone to bed and read for half an hour before putting the book away and switching off the light. Almost instantly you were asleep, the world you live in suddenly winked out. In deep sleep there was no awareness of anything, and time did not exist. You don't know how long you were asleep before you began to dream. The next thing you were aware of was hearing the alarm go off in your dream before starting on the hike to the glacier. The dream was as real to you as the world you inhabit in your waking hours.

The Taoist masters were aware of this phenomenon and posed the question: "Am I a butterfly dreaming I am a man, or am I a man dreaming I am a butterfly?" By what authority do we claim our waking state to be real while our dream state is not?

The Toltec shamans concluded that the waking state was a dream, a dream as real as those experienced at night. What happens is that we're conditioned by those around us to believe that the waking state is real and the dreaming state unreal. In this way we create a preference for the "waking" state, which becomes the reality against which all other states are compared. We learn this as part of the acculturation process, the process by which we come to accept the basic assumptions of the culture within which we are raised. What the shamans did was to dislodge the certainty we have in the waking state while at the same time teaching the acolyte the underlying assumptions that operate in the so-called dream world. Having mastered the underlying premises of the dream world, the shamans were able to function as skillfully there as in the waking world. For most of us, however, the conditioning is strong enough that we rarely question the reality of the waking world and therefore consider the dream state nothing but an illusion.

When we fall asleep at night, the experience is something like having the lights turned out, as awareness of the waking world vanishes. When we enter the dream world, it's as if the light of consciousness is suddenly switched on again; it can be so real that we're incapable of distinguishing between the dream and waking states. When we awaken from deep sleep we enter the waking world, and the experience is of the light of consciousness being switched on again.

Another way to describe what takes place is that when we fall asleep we awaken into the dream world; then later, from the state of dreaming consciousness, we fall asleep and re-awaken into another dream world, the one we've been conditioned to call the real world.

Could it be that both worlds are equally real, equally unreal, equally illusory, equally a dream? Could it be that God dreams us into existence as instruments of consciousness? Could it also be that as instruments of consciousness God dreams, through us, both dream states? If this is true then it would suggest that the world we inhabit on a daily basis is as much an intermittent occurrence as the world of our dreams.

When we examine what is verifiable to us, our direct firsthand experience, we would only be able to say that the world exists when we wake up. We've absolutely no awareness of the world continuing while we're asleep. Our belief that the world continues to exist while asleep is based solely on two sources. The first is what others have told us: namely that they've seen us sleeping, and therefore the world must continue while we're asleep because they inhabit that world. The second source is our own observations of people sleeping while we're awake. There's a problem with both of these sources of information, however.

Our friends who've seen us sleeping are characters we are dreaming and can only be found in our dreams, whether they be the dreams of night or the living dream we take for reality. Our observation of friends sleeping while we're awake also takes place in our dreamed nights or days. No information is derived from any independent and verifiable source outside those dreams. How then, can we be sure the world has continuity, that it exists while we're in deep sleep even though we've no awareness of it? There's no way we can know that. What we're left with is a belief, and as was noted at the outset, beliefs are not fact or truth.

One of the major criteria for what is real is that which persists. Since neither the dreams at night nor the waking state can be said to persist, they would therefore be fundamentally illusory.

From this perspective God, it turns out, is the master dreamer, and all of us are characters in the dream created by God. Lao Tzu speaks of this when he says,

The heavens and the earth are unreal,
The ten thousand things an illusion.
To the sage, life's but a dream,
And all mankind
Characters dreamed by the Tao.

If this is true, if this is the nature of reality, then all the events that have taken place in the world throughout history, all the events taking place today, all the wars, conflict and terrorism, all the people making love and war, all the death and all the suffering, are really and truly an entertaining illusion within which each of us as dreamed characters gets to play the role assigned to us when the dream began. All of this, everything this book addresses is simply God's Lila, God's dance. What a relief. And as Ramana Maharshi said, "nothing ever happened."

The Divine movie

Another metaphor used to describe the world in which we live is the metaphor of the movie. The movie is a projection from the realm of possibilities onto the screen of consciousness. Another way of describing it is to say that consciousness not aware of itself becomes aware of itself as the potential energy becomes actualized. When we go to see a movie the action seems to be taking place as we watch it, although we know the movie has already been made.

The movie of life represents the actualization of one of an untold number of potential stories, so to speak. In order for the objects of the phenomenal world to be perceived, consciousness creates sentient objects capable of perception. The sentient object and the objects of perception are one single event, a single event in consciousness itself. The divine movie comes into existence through the projection of all sentient objects upon the screen of the Totality of Consciousness. Consider the possibility that what we take to be out there, the phenomenal world within which we appear to live, is actually a projection of an internal world, a world in here, within consciousness itself.

• • • I am—The womb of the universe

When I became an agnostic it was not a repudiation of God but rather a repudiation of what I thought to be an anthropomorphic projection of the ego to which the name of God had been applied. The idea that God was a glorified human being did not ring true. Christian teaching as found in the churches was, to say the least, immature, almost infantile. Other than the theology of Paul Tillich, I found little that made much sense. A more helpful understanding of God, however, emerged slowly and continued for many years, below the level of awareness.

An intermediate stage showed itself while I was staying at the ashram of Sai Baba. I'd been ill for four days. The heat was stifling, and in a semi-delirious manner I found myself contemplating the idea of God. Within my mental world a visual image appeared: a small pond had dried from intense heat. The mud at its bottom was cracked and curled. I noticed one piece raised more than the others. Looking closely I saw that a small green plant had pushed the cracked mud out of the way. What I realized from this was that God, the life force, was implicitly embedded in the universe. That life force, the divine energy, always found expression even in the most desolate places; there was absolutely no separation between the creative potential and the actual manifestation.

Years later I was driving from my home in Hawi to my work in Kealakekua. The issue of death suddenly entered my mind and I felt a sudden jolt, like someone about to die. I realized it is the ego that is afraid of death, afraid it will no longer exist. The amazing and laughable thing is that it really doesn't exist in the first place; the ego is simply a concept.

A couple of years later, I'd been home for a few days after returning from a trip to India. Our home was on the northern tip of the Big Island of Hawaii, at about five hundred feet above sea level. The house, in the middle of some cattle fields, was on the edge of an eroded grass-covered volcanic vent, and completely isolated from any other habitation, with ocean on three sides. On the night in question there was a full moon and the trade winds had stopped blowing, so it was quiet and calm. I'd fallen into a deep sleep.

During the night I woke up, and from my bed could see the moon reflecting off the water between Hawaii, and the volcano Haleakala, forty miles across the strait on Maui. As I lay there I became aware of a great deal of tension in my body. It was as if it was vibrating with a kind of restrained or restricted energy. It dawned on me that what I was aware of was the subtle vibrational energies that comprise the body itself. I noticed that everything vibrated—wood, stone, the grass in the surrounding fields, and flesh, all with characteristic vibrations peculiar to each of them. My wife was sleeping beside me and I could feel her vibrations as well. I found myself looking down at the bed, the house and the island, and it was as though I was looking deep into myself.

I found myself wondering, who was this me that was observing? Immediately the awareness came that the me was a kind of intense, circumscribed, strongly vibrating noise, which was somehow an unnecessary constriction of consciousness itself. The underlying consciousness was restricted by the structure of the personal consciousness, the me, the ego.

As I watched, the me dissolved, and as it did, I became aware that all I am, all I have ever been, and all I will ever be is awareness, consciousness itself. As this awareness took hold, I witnessed with a deep love and compassion all the people of the planet. They were like ants that crawled and scraped across this blue spinning home in the blackness of space. Each one exhibited the noisy cacophony of the egoic consciousness, bent on fulfilling its own intentions. It was obvious that part of God's Lila materialized from such a play of noise, the noise of the mind.

I witnessed the rise of conflict and war and saw how it was counter-balanced by peacemaking. In fact, yin and yang were everywhere in existence, everywhere at play, implicit, a tension of opposites holding the phenomenal world in place, including the mental aspects as well. Looking down at the earth it was possible to feel the tension, the collective vibrational forces of the life of the planet, and around it and above it the discordant yet natural energy of the collective egoic consciousness.

As I continued to observe, the planet receded and there was a sense that galaxies came spiraling out of me, out of the Totality of Consciousness, I am. Then just as I had witnessed them emerging they dissolved into me again. This happened again and again. It was as if they were born out of my belly and returned to it. I was both the potential and actual consciousness. From the void that I am, universes were being born and the world of form emerged and vanished deep within me.

The awareness that all there is, is consciousness, that all there has ever been is consciousness, that all there will ever be is consciousness, and that I am that, was unshakable. It was a fact, and I'd always known this; it was written in the very heart of my being, and then, somehow forgotten, obscured by the personal consciousness I'd mistaken for myself. This consciousness had characteristics not noticed before. It was alive, the source of all life, it was love; vibrant, tangible, intensely real, greater than the reality of the world of phenomena which emerged from it.

The irony of it struck me deeply, and I found myself laughing quietly. It was so simple, yet I'd missed it all those years; and now the underlying nature of reality was revealed in all its awesome simplicity. It was what I am and what I have always been. This of course is true for all human beings, all life forms, without exception, whether realized or not. The sense of I am is not personal but impersonal and universal. The experience, if that is what it could be called, was one of profound compassion, of an unshakable immovable love that has never not existed.

Death had become irrelevant, simply an illusion. All there had ever been and all there ever would be was life, consciousness itself; and within it all, the ego would make its billions of appearances and disappearances, like winking lights over the vast expanses of space and time.

A deep and abiding peacefulness had come upon me. I fell into a sound sleep, and when I awoke in the morning the peace and awareness remained.

*Talk to some people about these things
and they'll lock you up.*
Ramesh Balsekar

Chapter 22
Not Veranda Talk

Be warned

Ramesh would sometimes warn us about talking indiscriminately with people concerning the things discussed in his presence. "This is not veranda talk," he would say. "Talk to some people about these things and they'll lock you up."

Christ stated the same thing more bluntly when he said, "Cast not your pearls before swine."

You wish to help?

The following story is adapted from the Sufi tradition. Horris was an observant man and his keen mind saw possibilities others did not. Shortly after the invention of the wheel he was sitting on the side of the road when four oxen came by, pulling a heavy cart. Smoke was pouring from one of the wheels. The driver stopped, jumped down and as he approached the smoking wheel it burst into flames. Horris helped the driver put the fire out.

When Horris got home he went to his workshop and attaching a wheel to a wooden axle, produced the same result. By the end of the month he'd produced a smaller version of the same idea, a machine capable of creating fire.

Besides being observant, Horris had a warm and generous heart, and this quality took him on the road. He wanted to teach people how to make fire for themselves and how to use it. He set out across the country to talk to the five tribes. It took him a year. People were impressed with his invention. But, the idea of fire did not sit well with everybody.

The major industry in the country revolved around raising sheep and producing woolen sweaters and blankets. With the advent of fire, business declined. Defiance amongst the wool-growers and sweater-makers grew, and the people who might have benefited were whipped into a frenzy of opposition based on the clever use of lies and half-truths. One day Horris was found in a ditch; he'd been murdered.

Two hundred years later a sage and his disciples were crossing the country and traveled through the five tribal regions. When they entered the first they found that fire was used by the priests in elaborate rituals. The priests, privy to the secrets of fire, used it to heat their homes while the common people froze.

Arriving in the second tribal territory, they found the knowledge of making fire was present, but the ability to make it was lacking. The religious chants of this tribe contained detailed instructions on how to make fire. None of the people understood their significance, however, and as a result they spent cold winters in unheated houses.

When the travelers crossed into the third tribal area they noticed in front of each of the homes a wooden idol bearing the resemblance of a man and the name Horris inscribed on the pedestal. In this tribe, religion was centered on myths—one in particular, an epic of Horris, the bringer of fire. Fire was worshiped by all and understood by only a few.

Arriving in the fourth tribal area, the small band of wanderers found the people had replicas of the instrument of fire. Large ones had been put in the churches where they were worshiped. Information on fire was secondhand and was of the status of myth. No one had ever seen fire, however, because Horris had died before he reached the tribe.

To their surprise the little band discovered that the fifth tribe was not only familiar with fire but knew how to use it. They cooked their meals and, in the winter, heated their homes. They'd learned of fire from a friend of Horris who'd moved north to escape the "Troubles," concerning who should control fire following the death of Horris.

Stopping to rest under a tree, the master and his disciples reflected upon what they'd seen. One of the disciples noted that in each tribe fire was a central theme, but in the first four regions its usefulness for humanity was obscured. "Because we know about fire and its uses, should we not teach this knowledge to those who don't have it? Surely life would be much easier if the people understood how to make and use fire." Some of the disciples nodded in agreement.

The master said, "If you really want to help, then we will repeat the journey and by the end of it you'll understand how difficult it is."

When they came to the first tribal area they were welcomed by the priests and treated hospitably. Their presence was requested at the most sacred ceremony of the year, the public making of fire.

Afterward, the master asked the disciples if anyone had anything to say. One of the disciples spoke up. "I feel it is my obligation to show the people that anyone can make fire, not just the priests."

The master responded. "You may do so if you feel compelled and are willing to take the consequences, whatever they are." The disciple agreed. He met with the priests and said to them: "If I can create fire like you, would you concede that you are not the only ones who can do so and that in fact the people can make it for themselves?"

The priests seized him and charged him with heresy. He was taken away in chains and never seen again.

The master and the disciples continued on their way. When they came to the second tribe they were welcomed and invited to participate in the chanting ceremonies, which included the instructions for making fire. After an evening of chants and ritual one of the disciples spoke up, having previously agreed to accept whatever consequences there might be. The people gathered in the great hall to hear what he had to say. "Your spiritual chants are really not spiritual at all, they are simply instructions on how to make and use fire. If you followed the instructions you'd be blessed with fire and could heat your homes in winter."

After a moment's silence one of the tribal elders stood and spoke. "We know you mean well, but you are strangers here. You don't know our customs and history, you barely understand our language and are presumptuous enough to think you can teach us. We decline your offer and will continue in our accustomed ways since they have served us well over the years.

The master and his disciples continued to the third tribe, where the likeness of Horris stood before each home. They were welcomed and invited to the temple where a large reclining image of Horris was the centerpiece of tribal worship. After the service one of the disciples addressed the people and said: "Horris was a man, and as such he represented the knowledge of a possibility. To bring that possibility forth is all that is important, not the worship of the image of a man." The hall went silent and then in unison the people stamped their feet, like a powerful drum beat, and with raised arms pointed north while chanting, "Begone."

When the travelers crossed the border into the land of the fourth tribe they encountered friendly people who welcomed them graciously. The small band spent several days of feasting and resting. On Sunday, they'd been invited as guest speakers to attend churches of the three denominations. Three of the disciples, seeing the invitation as an opportunity, were quick to accept the offer. The disciples shared a common message with the parishioners. "You don't know the use of the machine you worship; you don't understand what it can do, and how it can make your lives richer. The machine itself is not important, but the fire it was designed to produce is. We know how to make fire with it and can show you."

The most liberal of the congregations concluded that what they were told was the truth and so wanted to learn the creation and use of fire. When the master and disciples probed the motivation of the clergy, it turned out they were interested only because of the status it would confer upon them when the other denominations rejected the offer as they were sure to do. And, that's exactly what happened.

When the master and the disciples entered the fifth tribal area they could see the production and use of fire was routine, no longer a focus of attention. Now other things provided the focus.

The master gathered the disciples together and said: If you wish to teach, you have first to help people understand there is something to learn. And when they understand there is something to learn, you have to direct them to learn what they need to learn, not what they think they should learn. Having understood this you may begin to teach. But, understanding alone is not enough to make an effective teacher. The teacher must have the capacity to teach in such a way as to tickle in his students the awareness of truth, so that when the student scratches the itch, understanding takes place. That capacity, however, is rare.

As of old
When a man awakens to reality
The nature of the universe lies revealed.

Consciousness gives birth to the ten thousand things
And the same Consciousness perceives them.

Without Consciousness
The stars would fall from the heavens
Galaxies would fly apart
The earth would be flung from its orbit
And the valleys, teeming with life
Would shrivel and die.
Even the idea of God would no longer exist.

Lao Tzu

Chapter 23
The Old Man

Only the truth is the truth—believe it or not

I'd been searching for many years; to no avail. I'd been told it was in a particular region of the country and when I found myself there one autumn I looked for it. Walking along the street I saw a large stone cathedral on the left. I made my way to the office of the minister, and was soon seated in a comfortable chair in the minister's office. He seemed like a nice enough fellow, and after the usual pleasantries I came out with the question that would not let me go. I explained what I was looking for and as I did he nodded his head. At last, I thought, I've found someone who knows.

Having received detailed instructions I

left the sanctuary and started on my way. My heart was light and a sense of eager anticipation buoyed my steps. It took only a matter of minutes but at last I neared my objective. I got out of the taxi and thanked the driver. I was close. At the bottom of the road was a sharp right turn and I'd been assured I'd find what I was looking for a few hundred yards further along.

Rounding the corner I was fairly running. I stopped, taken aback. This was not what I was looking for. Deflated I walked back along the crowded sidewalk. What had gone wrong? Had I misunderstood the directions? I noticed a large synagogue to my right. Similar to the cathedral in size, it lacked the large spire on its towers. Maybe the rabbi would know.

I turned the handle and pushed on the small door, recessed into the large main door. It swung inward with a bit of a squeak. My eyes adjusted to the subdued light as I walked toward the far end of the building. A rabbi appeared from a connecting passage. He came over extending his hand and with a friendly smile asked, "Can I help?" I certainly hoped he could.

We sat in the pews next to each other and I explained the nature of my business. The rabbi asked several questions and by the end of the conversation seemed to have a clear understanding as to the nature of my search. More encouraging was the smile on his face and the way he nodded his head; this man obviously knew. I listened carefully to the rabbi's instructions and even took notes. When he finished I thanked him for his time and left.

Outside, darkness was approaching and I thought it best to wait until the next day to continue the search. In the morning I arose early, showered, dressed and entered the hotel restaurant for a hearty breakfast. An hour later, as a low sun sent shafts of light between tall buildings, I sped toward my destination. After giving careful directions to the taxi driver, I was assured that he too knew the place I was looking for. Encouraged, I sat back and enjoyed the scenery. Before long we'd left the city and turned onto a small lane that led deep into the countryside.

It was mid-morning when we arrived in a small village and pulled up to a pair of old iron gates. They formed the entrance to a beautiful public garden. "Follow the path," the driver instructed me, "and you'll find what you've been looking for." Then with a cheery wave he turned and sped away.

The garden was beautiful and well cared for, with a shaded walkway ending on the shore of a small lake. Beautiful as it was, it was not what I'd been looking for. Deeply disappointed I retraced my steps until I came to a restaurant. I stopped for an early lunch. When I was finished I asked the waiter if he knew where I might find what I was looking for. "No, I'm sorry, I don't know about such things," he said, "but there's a Tibetan temple a mile beyond the village, perhaps they could help." I thanked him, picked up my bag and followed his directions.

Before long the temple came into view. I rang the bell that hung beside a door in the high wall surrounding the temple grounds. The door opened and an ochre-clad man with shaved head stood before me. I explained the nature of my business; he nodded and ushered me into a courtyard and directed me to a seat beside a small fountain. "Someone will be with you in a moment," he said.

I liked the peacefulness of the grounds and, closing my eyes, became aware of the chirping of birds and the gentle splash of water on rocks. When I opened them again, another similarly clad man was seated before me. A little older than the one who'd first greeted me, he smiled and bowed slightly, asking how he could help.

After explaining the nature of my search the older man took my hands in his and, gazing into my eyes, gave me detailed instructions on how to find what I was looking for. When he'd finished he asked several questions to make sure I'd clearly understood and then showed me to the door that led from the temple grounds.

Turning right, I followed the lane away from the village and down a gently sloping hill, which crossed a low valley before climbing steeply into a heavily forested area. By late afternoon I arrived at a quaint bridge beneath which a stream tumbled on its way to the valley below. Crossing the bridge I noticed a small cabin nestled amongst some trees on a low hill beside the singing water. Beautiful as it was, it was not what I was looking for. Once more I was disappointed. Why had those people I'd asked spoken with such authority about something they obviously knew nothing about?

I sat on a rock beside the stream and listened to its many voices. Somehow it soothed my mind. I don't know how long I sat there but when I looked up I saw an old man coming toward me along the path from the cabin. Without saying a word he seated himself beside me. We sat thus for at least an hour. Dusk had fallen when he reached out a large hand to mine and turning toward me said, "You will stay the night and tomorrow we'll see what happens." I got up and followed him to the cabin. By candlelight we cleaned, peeled and chopped vegetables, and cooked rice over a small wood stove, which also warmed the cabin on this now chilly evening.

After a good night's sleep I went to the stream to wash. The cold water was refreshing, and when I finished I turned to see the old man standing with a rough towel for my use. Taking the towel, I thanked him; he nodded and returned to the cabin.

Over tea and a bowl of fruit the old man asked what I was looking for. When I told him he inquired, "Have you found it?" "No" I said and then described the frustrating nature of my search. As he nodded his head I was certain he understood. "Do you know where I can find what I'm looking for?" I impulsively asked. In his eyes I could see an utter tranquility, something I'd never seen in anyone before. He said nothing. "Do you?" I persisted. With a slight nod of his head and what looked like a smile he spoke a few brief words and was silent again. When I questioned him further he did not respond. I stayed with him a couple of days soaking in the silence before it was time to leave.

With a backward glance and a wave of the hand I crossed the bridge early one morning. Did the old man know the truth, the whereabouts of what I sought? I didn't think so. Why would the old man's directions be any more accurate than anyone else's?

Years later I found myself in the same part of the country where my search had come to an end. Over the years I'd thought often about the mysterious old man who lived in a cabin beside the tumbling stream. Had he really known where I could find what I was looking for? Were his directions accurate? It was late one afternoon when I found myself following the lane as it climbed out of the low valley and into the dense forest. Locating the tall cedar the old man had told me of, I followed a barely discernible trail, which after half an hour opened into a large glade lit by a low sun reflecting off a tall sand-colored rock face. And there it was, what I'd been looking for all my life. The old man had been right.

The way is so simple
People find it hard to accept.

It is easier for them to believe
That life is complex
Difficult and confusing.

Lao Tzu

Glossary

What follows are definitions of key words as used by the author throughout this book.

A priori: Something which has to exist in order for something else to exist. For example; light produces the possibility of a shadow but does not guarantee it. Yet, without light the possibility of a shadow is non existent. It could be said that a shadow is dependent for its existence on light while light is not dependent on a shadow.

Advaita: Not two: Non duality, Absolute Unity; One, the Whole. Suggesting there is only one power, not two, as for example in the idea of God and the Devil. From the perspective of non-duality the subject and object can only occur together; each is essential for the other, therefore they are, in fact, part of a whole or totality.

Asanas: Yoga postures

Ashram: In the Hindu tradition an ashram was a hermitage where sages lived, but the meaning has since evolved into a kind of organized commune around a spiritual master. It's a place where spiritual seekers ask questions, engage in dialogue and conversation with a master and each other.

Attachment: Having to have the object of one's desire. Possessed by desire.

Belief: Accepting something to be true without really knowing if it's true or not. Belief is therefore rooted in uncertainty and ignorance; fundamental doubt exists and the underlying truth, whatever it is, remains obscured.

Bhakti Yoga: A spiritual path that leads to the dissolution of the egoic or personal consciousness and the restoration of the underlying impersonal consciousness. It generally involves spiritual practices such as those found in prayer and meditation, chants, the Japanese Tea Ceremony, the practice of sumi-e, calligraphy, dance etc. Devotional in nature it can take the form of worship of the divine power or God: when the guru is present love and devotion for the guru come into play. It is called the path of love and love is the ultimate teacher that leads to selflessness—the dissolution of the ego.

Conceptual: Having to do with ideas and language. For instance the word "rock" is conceptual, while the rock itself, is actual.

Conceptual duality: The use of language to express an idea that can only be defined in relationship to its opposite. For example, the concept of beauty is meaningless in the absence of ugliness.

Consciousness: The awareness of being; the sense of presence, of being alive. That within which the phenomenal world, the world of form, appears.

Cultural Hypnosis: The acceptance of cultural cues, assumptions and beliefs without awareness that this has happened and without awareness of what they are. This is an ongoing process, which causes and maintains the state referred to as: endarkenment, illusion, ignorance and confusion.

Darshan: It is used to describe the semi formal gatherings in the master's presence for the purpose of spiritual guidance.

Dualism: Occurs when a human being asserts one aspect of the two poles which comprise a single unit. For example good and bad define each other. To choose the good and reject the bad creates a conflict that cannot be resolved. Why? Because like the head and tail of a coin, good and bad are not separate, simply the extremes along a single continuum. This is why those who attempt to be exclusively good, must fail.

Duality: Includes conceptual duality as well. Duality is the observation that all objects in the phenomenal world are defined by their presence and absence. For example a rock is defined by that which is not rock and as such is capable of perception.

Ego: The personal aspect of consciousness associated with a particular body that suggests, by inference, the existence of a person, or some-one.

Endarkenment process: The process whereby the human being learns the cues, beliefs and fundamental assumptions concerning life within a particular culture. Acculturation. It represents the obscuring of the original awareness, the impersonal consciousness present at birth. Endarkenment also suggests its opposite, enlightenment.

Enlightenment: The permanent dissolution of the ego or personal consciousness associated with a particular body. Awakening from the state produced by the endarkenment process.

Existence: An object, appearing in consciousness capable of being percieved by the senses. It can also suggest the awareness of being, the awareness of presence, of being alive.

Free will: The belief that the human being can do anything he wishes; that he can accomplish whatever he sets out to accomplish through choices he makes freely; that he can do this without events, conditioning, thoughts and emotions influencing the decision making process in any way.

God: The First Cause, the Unmoved Mover, Potential Energy and its Actualization, the Source and Manifestation of Form. A concept representing the Unknown; the Great Mystery, or the Void.

Hubris: Overweening pride. Blinded by arrogance without awareness that this has happened.

Japa: Repeating, muttering as it were, a repetitive phrase as a form of anchor or focal point; a place to return after being distracted during meditation. It can also include for example, the counting of beads as found in the Catholic tradition of the rosary.

Jnanna yoga: The yoga of direct understanding or wisdom. It is a path to enlightenment that leads to the dissolution of the ego purely through deep understanding and without the necessity for spiritual practices. Zen, Taoism and Advaita Vedanta, are considered unique expressions of jnanna yoga. Though culturally and linguistically distinct, they point to the same observation concerning the underlying nature of reality.

Kahuna: Hawaiian shaman.

Karma: The idea of cause and effect.

Karma yoga: The practice of service; leading to selfless service, which culminates when the ego dies.

Mandala: Usually a visual pattern of some form used in meditation. The sand paintings practiced by the Tibetans is one example. It can be a stylized or geometric pattern derived from sacred geometry upon which the attention is placed to bring about the stilling of the mind.

Manifestation: The world around us, the world of objects, the world of the senses; from trees to galaxies.

Matrix: An underlying pattern that produces behavior.

Neophyte: Someone who is just beginning, someone unpracticed, someone in the early stages of learning.

Phenomenal: The world of form, of objects manifested to the senses, the physical reality of life.

Polarity: Has to do with poles, the idea of opposites and the natural dynamic tension between them; the spectrum between two extremes.

Polarize: To increase tension between two poles. It comes from the belief that one of two points of view is right and the other wrong. The idea that one should dominate the other, or that one alone should exist.

Responsibility: The ability to respond appropriately in a natural and spontaneous manner to whatever occurs.

Sanyassin: Spiritual practitioner, a follower of a particular school of thought or guru.

Sat Guru: An enlightened guru that enables the disciple to awaken by stimulating an awareness of the truth already present in him. It can also be used to point to the truth resident in all human beings.

Source: That which gives rise to something. The actualization of potential energy, often referred to as God, Allah, the Void, or the Tao.

Taoism: A description of life and how it works as first expressed by the Chinese sage, Lao Tzu, twenty-five hundred years ago. His description can be found in the collection of poems titled the "The Tao Te Ching," one of the great spiritual classics of all time.

Truth: Fact

Vedanta: The culmination of knowledge, the highest and final understanding of human nature and life as found in Hinduism, and derived from the Vedas.

Vedas: The oldest Hindu spiritual texts purported to hold the highest form of insight, awareness and wisdom. They are derived from an oral tradition that emerged from Indian culture and was first written down some five thousand years ago. They comprise the underlying philosophical explanations of life.

Vibhuti: Sacred ash used in Hinduism. Somewhat similar to the Christian use of water in rituals.

Vipassana: To see things as they are. A form of meditation that enables the practitioner to experience life as it is. This happens as the influence of the ego wanes.

Yin and Yang: ☯ The concept of opposites held in dynamic tension as for instance in male and female, good and bad, up and down. Harmony comes when the natural tension between the opposites spontaneously come to a state of balance. In that balance peace is to be found, almost as a by-product.

Yoga: One of a number of spiritual paths or disciplines leading to enlightenment.

*All quotes from Lao Tzu are taken from the book, **Something To Ponder, reflections from Lao Tzu's Tao Te Ching**, by Colin Mallard.*

Colin Mallard, Ph.D.

A love of ideas thrust him into a deep exploration of Western philosophy. He was convinced that the world in which we live is not quite as it appears. He also had a deep desire to understand himself and thus, by extension, all human beings. This intense search introduced him to Eastern philosophy and ultimately took him to India. He had the good fortune to study with the French Advaita Master, Dr. Jean Klein and the Indian Advaita master, Ramesh S. Balsekar who became his guru. Ramesh was able to destroy his pre-conceived notions and in the emptiness that remained the underlying reality emerged.